Joel

BIBLE STUDY COMMENTARY

Joel

RONALD B. ALLEN

Lamplighter Books Grand Rapids, Michigan
Zondervan Publishing House

BIBLE STUDY COMMENTARY: JOEL
Copyright © 1988 by Ronald B. Allen

Lamplighter Books are published by the Zondervan Publishing House
1415 Lake Drive, S.E., Grand Rapids, Michigan 49506

Library of Congress Cataloging-in-Publication Data

Allen, Ronald Barclay.
   Joel : Bible study commentary / Ronald B. Allen.
     p. cm. – (Bible study commentary series)

"Lamplighter books."
Bibliography: p.
ISBN 0-310-41721-X
   1. Bible. O.T. Joel—Commentaries. I. Title. II. Series.
BS1575.3.A44   1988
224'.707—dc19   88–11785
                                                     CIP

Edited by Nia Jones, John Sloan

Printed in the United States of America

88 89 90 91 92 93 / CH / 10 9 8 7 6 5 4 3 2 1

For my daughter, Laureen Elizabeth,
with much love.

Contents

Contents

Foreword

There is nothing quite as satisfying for the student as discovering a new portion of the Scripture—its riches of truth and its beauty of expression. It is my prayer for you that your study of the Book of Joel will be a special discovery of joy.

Because of the relative brevity, but profound importance, of the little Book of Joel, I have included some application-discussion materials, especially concerning the issues of the locust invasion, the meaning of the Day of Yahweh, and the inclusive aspects of the prophecy of the outpouring of the Holy Spirit.

I have referred to the New International Version of the Holy Bible as the principal English text in this commentary. I have taken the liberty to make one change consistently when I have quoted from that text: Wherever the NIV has "the LORD" I have substituted "Yahweh," the Hebrew name for God.

At times I quote other English translations of the Bible. The King James Version (1611) is identified as KJV; the New King James Version (1982), as NKJV; and the New American Standard Bible, as NASB.

The Hebrew text from which I make citations is the current scholarly edition of the Masoretic text, *Biblia Hebraica Stuttgartensia*, edited by K. Elliger and W. Rudolph.

May God's Spirit, promised by Joel, bless your study!

Chapter 1

Introduction to the Book

Joel and the *Minor Prophets*

An unintended slight renders twelve biblical books nearly to the netherworld of Christian consciousness. The Latin designation "Minor" ascribed to twelve of the Hebrew prophets means "small" or "short," in comparison to the "Major" (that is, longer) prophetic books. Practically, the word "minor" has been regarded to mean unimportant or insignificant. We are all the losers in this misunderstanding. Christian readers who tend to treat the Old Testament as a distant, unknown sea may regard these twelve little books as the truly murky waters. So they may think that it doesn't matter much if they don't read these books; after all, these are the "minor" books. But they really are not "minor," only short by comparison with Isaiah or Jeremiah.

During ancient times, all biblical writings were in the form of scrolls. Because of the relative brevity of these twelve books, the Hebrew textual scholars, the scribes, either wrote them on one longer than average scroll or stored them together in one drawer in the temple archives. In this way the Hebrew custom developed to refer to this collection of twelve short prophetic books as *The Twelve*. From the study of Hebrew Scripture and Jewish tradition, one learns to speak of this collection as The Twelve. However, few Christians have learned to use this appropriate title for the "Minor Prophets."

Perhaps we may bring some change of image for these books among Christian people if we move away from the Latin

11

term "Minor" and replace it with a more understandable English word, such as "shorter." If we learn to speak of these twelve books as the "Shorter Prophetic Books" (not "Shorter Prophets," or we introduce another problem!), we may enhance their appeal among modern readers.

For the books are *not* minor; in fact, the twelve shorter prophetic books have great significance in the record of God's dealing with his people. Each of these is a unique contribution to the whole of biblical truth. Interestingly enough, they vary in subject matter, in time, in style, and in message. Even their brevity enhances our present study of them. It seems to be far better to begin our study of a small prophetic book, such as Joel, and learn to swim in its waters than to dive headlong into a much longer prophetic book such as Jeremiah, and flounder, with no clear idea even of the direction to shore.

The Message of Joel

The second of The Twelve is the Book of Joel, our shorter prophetic book for this study. Only three chapters long, the little Book of Joel presents a significant number of problems for us to face in its interpretation, although the overall message of the book is clear enough. And the importance of his message is as vital in our day as when he first preached the word of Yahweh.

The prophet Joel, whose name means "Yahweh is God," speaks insightfully about the reality of God in everyday life, vividly about the Judgment Day, and gloriously about the future promise of God for the redemption and renewal of his people Israel. Significant elements in the Book of Joel include his emphasis upon the concept of the Day of Yahweh (or "the Day of the LORD," see author's foreword) and his portrayal of the Holy Spirit's outpouring in the latter days. We will examine each of these themes in this study commentary.

The Two-fold Structure of the Book of Joel

The three chapters of the Book of Joel may be divided into two nearly equal sections of thirty-seven and thirty-five verses each. The first part of the book is centered during the present and near future of the author in a context of calamity and terrible judgment (1:2–2:17). The second section of the book speaks of

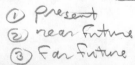
① present
② near future
③ far future

the far future, extending to the establishment of the kingdom of God on earth (2:18–3:21).

We may note that the chapter divisions in our Bibles are not very helpful to us, since they do not really present the fundamental structure of the book. As in the case of some other Scriptures, it is sometimes a good practice of Bible study to ignore the chapter divisions when looking for the structure of a book and to decide only to use them as a means of finding one's location. The well-known Bible expositor Dr. Ray Stedman of Peninsula Bible Church in Palo Alto, California, has remarked facetiously, "God inspired the text; the Devil gave us the chapter divisions."

The principal speaker in the first section of the Book of Joel is the prophet; Yahweh speaks more directly in the second. Joel moves from a natural calamity of a plague of locusts when the land was stripped of produce (see 1:4) to a glorious future day when the land will be overwhelmed with plenty because of the presence and blessing of the God of creation (see 3:18). These two sections serve not only as an explanation of God's workings in the historical present and in the prophetic future but also as a beautiful literary purpose of aesthetic wholeness. While the Scripture is to be our source of instruction, it may also be a source of enjoyment.

Here is a brief outline of the book to be expanded in the study commentary that follows.

  I. The title of the book. (Joel 1:1)
 II. The plague of locusts, a foreboding warning of the approaching Day of Yahweh. (Joel 1:2–2:17)
III. The promise of Yahweh to renew his land and to bless his people in a spectacular manner. (Joel 2:18–3:21)

The Plague of Locusts

In the first major section of the book, the prophet Joel seizes upon an unprecedented natural calamity to the city of Jerusalem and the nation of Judah, which bears witness to the sheer awesomeness of the devastation by a plague of locusts.

> What the locust swarm has left
>   the great locusts have eaten;
> what the great locusts have left
>   the young locusts have eaten;
> what the young locusts have left
>   other locusts have eaten (1:4).

The land was laid so low by the all-consuming band of insects in their terrifying invasion that Joel calls out to various groups who will be affected by the destruction of agriculture. He calls to those who love wine to weep, since the vineyards have been destroyed. Not only will there not be a good year for wine this year, there will be *no* year for wine this year! (1:5–7).

But the severely affected palates of those given to wine are just the beginning of sorrow, for offerings in the Temple will be affected as well. How may a person bring a wine offering to Yahweh or an offering of grain when

> The fields are ruined,
>   the ground is dried up;
> the grain is destroyed,
>   the new wine is dried up,
>   the oil fails (1:10).

Farmers (1:11–12) and priests (1:13–16) are affected alike. The destruction of agriculture will bring no joy to the growers nor to those who minister before the Lord with the produce.

On the basis of this terrible catastrophe, Joel considers the coming Day of Yahweh. So the events of the recent past forced him to think of the events in the near future. He reasons that the people have not seen anything yet.

> What a dreadful day!
>   For the day of Yahweh is near;
>   it will come like destruction from
> the Almighty (1:15).

Joel himself empathizes with the suffering of his people and his nation in those hard days. He prays to the Lord in words reminiscent of a psalm of lament (such as Psalm 142). As a result of the destruction of agriculture, there is a lack of water and a flame to the fields. Man and beast are endangered, and the troubles are only beginning (1:19–20).

From the present distress, the prophet slips again into the

coming trouble of the Day of the Lord. He speaks of the approaching day in much the same terms as does the prophet Zephaniah (Zeph. 1:14–16). It is a day of extraordinary darkness, and it is soon coming (Joel 2:1–2). It is also a day of terrible fire, a fire that devours and destroys and leaves no hope and no help (2:3). Following the fire comes an avenging army of invincible power and awesome might (2:2–10). The worst possible thing about this terrible army is that Yahweh himself is directing their victories. Heaven and earth are affected; when Yahweh roars, the army comes.

> The day of Yahweh is great;
> it is dreadful.
> Who can endure it? (2:11, last lines).

The only rational reaction to these words of coming judgment is a thorough revival, a complete national repentance. From babies to aged men, the entire nation needs to repent. Priests need to weep; brides and their bridegrooms need to delay their honeymoons. Why should the nations be allowed to say about a destroyed and unrepentant people,

> " 'Where is their God?' " (2:17, last line).

Despite the great wickedness of the people of Judah, there still may be time to avert something far worse than these devouring little insects. Even though the locusts were a ravaging of God's creation, the coming judgment of God will be beyond the experience of the planet. Nevertheless, there is still hope for mercy.

> Who knows? He may turn and have pity
> and leave behind a blessing—
> grain offerings and drink offerings
> for Yahweh your God (2:14).

The Promise of Yahweh

The second major section of the Book of Joel begins with the words of Yahweh himself in Joel 2:19. In spite of the terrible destruction of agriculture in the present plague, when there is neither wine to drink nor offerings to give to the Lord, there will

be an abundance of plenty in the days of blessing to come.
Yahweh states,

> "I am sending you grain, new wine and oil,
>   enough to satisfy you fully;
> never again will I make you
>   an object of scorn to the nations" (2:19).

God's promise of plenty extends to man and beast; his
provision from pasture to forest. Rain will come in abundance,
then the people will eat in plenty and give great praise to God.
The words of the prophet concerning the terrible locust invasion
(1:4) are used by the Lord in his reversal of evil to good.

> I will repay you for the years the
>   locusts have eaten—
>   the great locust and the young locust,
>   the other locusts and the locust swarm—
> my great army that I sent among you (2:25).

The day of the renewal will be marked by the presence of
the Lord himself in the midst of his people (2:27) and the
outpouring of his Holy Spirit on all his people (2:28–29). This
will be a day of wonders in heaven and signs on earth,
particularly a day of salvation and redemption (2:30–32).

These events of wonder will be associated with the
regathering of the people of God, the great battle of God against
all his enemies in the Valley of Jehoshaphat (3:1–15). Again,
Yahweh will roar; the heavens will shake.

> But Yahweh will be a refuge for his people,
>   a stronghold for the people of Israel (3:16, last half).

Yahweh will live in the midst of his people in the holy city
of Jerusalem (3:17). Agriculture will be renewed to the state of
the primordial Garden of Eden. The fate of the enemies is
sealed. The blessing of God is sure, for in that day it will be said,

> Yahweh dwells in Zion! (3:21, last line).

These are the themes of the splendid prophetic shorter
Book of Joel. They are grand themes, ones that we will pursue
more thoroughly in the study commentary to follow.

For Further Study

1. Even though there is some misunderstanding over the word "minor" in the Minor Prophets, there are some books of the Bible that are "key" or "central" books. What do you regard as the principal Old and New Testament books, and why do you regard these in this manner? Are any of the "Minor Prophets" among them? Is the Book of Joel one of them?

2. When some books are defined as "central" or "key" books, what effect does that have on the biblical canon? That is, if some books are not key or central, what loss would there be if they were excluded or lost?

3. What practical loss is there when some books are ignored, never read? Some people might be willing to die to protect the whole Bible, but they are not interested in taking the trouble to read large parts of that Scripture.

4. Joel's name has a significant meaning. How many of the writing prophets have names whose Hebrew meaning you know or can discover? You may wish to look up these names in a Bible dictionary.

Chapter 2

The Prophet Joel and His Times

Reading a Prophet

Our understanding of a biblical book is often greatly
enhanced when we have an adequate knowledge of the writer
and his times. The extended story of the life of David, for
example, affords numerous salient insights into selected David-
ic psalms. A text such as Psalm 63 is given a dramatic context by
the setting suggested by its superscription, "When he was in the
desert of Judah." The opening words of this psalm present
David's spirit thirsting for God much as his body longs for water
in a dry and weary land (see Ps. 63:1). A knowledge of David's
sojourn in the wilderness deeply amplifies our appreciation of
the words in his poem.

The prophets also help to explain themselves and their
messages by interrelating their messages with their times. The
Book of Jonah is intensely biographical; the message of the book
is the message of the prophet's life. Even the better known
prophetic writers set their lives and times in the flow of their
message. The life of Jeremiah is deftly interwoven into the
fabric of his book. We can appreciate the details of the prophet's
message because he presents so personally his relationship to
the people and his involvement in their setting. Jeremiah's
message is made more real to us because we sense the reality of
his person in the telling.

Unfortunately, in the case of the prophet Joel we have very
little information about his person and no certainty at all

concerning the times in which he lived. Outside of some
personality and place indicators we may gather from the tone
and literary features of his book, we really know very little about
the author of the Book of Joel.

All that we know for certain comes in the first verse of the
book.

> The word of Yahweh that came to
> Joel son of Pethuel (1:1).

In this verse we have precious little to go on, so our going
should be slow and deliberate. What we have is his name and
the notice that the message was from a true prophet of Yahweh.

The Prophet's Name

The name Joel is a type of name common in Israel. A form
of a term for deity is combined with another word to express the
faith that the parents desired to be realized in their child. We
call these names theophoric, built on forms of the names of God.

In Joel's name two different divine designations are combined: a short form of the name of God, Yahweh, and the
singular form for the basic word of God, 'ēl. His name means
"Yahweh is God." Such a name is a bold attestation of robust
faith in the God of reality. During this time, there were
questions concerning the exclusive demands of the God of
Israel as well as unbelief and uncertainty about the reality and
the identity of the true God. The name Joel is quite similar in
function to the name of the prophet Elijah, where the two
elements are reversed: "My God is Yahweh."

Joel also names his father, Pethuel, who is otherwise
unknown. This name, also theophoric, may mean something
such as "God is spacious." The first element pethu may come
from the verb pātâ, meaning "to be open," "to be spacious."
The designation "Joel son of Pethuel" ("x son of y") is actually a
way of stating a man's name. Long before there were family
names, an individual would be known as "x son of y" to
distinguish him from "x son of z."

The Prophet's Word

The first verse informs us that he was a true prophet of
Yahweh and that his message had its origin in God. The wording

of the Hebrew text is dramatic in its simplicity, "the word of Yahweh which was (or which came) to Joel son of Pethuel." This same type of phrasing is found in Hosea 1:1, Micah 1:1, and Zephaniah 1:1. Other prophetic books also begin with some variation on this language.

This heading reminds us of the more expressive account that comes in the larger book of the prophet Jeremiah who records his vision of the reception of God's message. Jeremiah initially resisted the divine commission of prophet, as had Moses long before his day. In the context of interchange between Yahweh's call and Jeremiah's resistance, we read of a bold gesture wherein the reluctant prophet sensed the outstretched hand of Yahweh touching his mouth. God says, "Now, I have put my words in your mouth" (Jer. 1:9). I find these words to be quite impressive for our understanding of the prophetic reception of the words of God.

The prophets were not dictation machines, who listened to a sentence from heaven, wrote it down, then waited for the next sentence to come. I cannot visualize a prophet saying, "Wait a moment, Lord, my pen just snapped. Would you go over that last line more slowly? How do you spell that name?"

We do believe that the prophets spoke as the Spirit of God gave them direction and that the message of the prophets came from God. But the process was as dynamic as it was mysterious. In the simplest of ways the prophets just say that the words of God came to them, then they gave voice to these words through their own mouths and written expression by their own pens.

The historic, orthodox view of Scripture is that it is thoroughly the work of God and fully the work of man— conjointly. The origin is of God; the expression, of man; the result, the very text the Spirit desired to be expressed.

So our prophet Joel states simply the mystery of the word of Yahweh in his life: The word of Yahweh was, that is came, to me.

The Prophet's World

The contents of the book indicate that Joel was a citizen of Judah and a resident of Jerusalem. He had significant interests in the work of the priests in the temple (see 1:8–10; 13–14;

2:17). And throughout his book he showed considerable knowledge of agriculture in all of its forms. It is possible that he was a true prophet of Yahweh associated specifically with the worship of God in the temple.

More than this we cannot say.

The Prophet's Times

Even more troubling is the matter of the time of his life and ministry. Many prophets specifically date their books during the reign of various kings of Israel and Judah (see Isa. 1:1; Jer. 1:1–3; Hos. 1:1; Amos 1:2). But the Book of Joel bears no name of king or date, no celestial happening, no battle scene that might be correlated with extra-biblical historical memory. Since there is not a hint for date of the Book of Joel in the text, we may not even say with certainty that the book is pre- or post-exilic. The worship problems he describes in the temple are not those of a Canaanite religious nature (suggesting a pre-exilic date), nor are they of a clash with, say, the proto-Samaritan sect (suggesting a post-exilic date).

Given this situation, it should be no surprise to learn that many scholars betray considerable diversity and not a little uncertainty when they speak of the date of this book. In some books of the Bible, the dating of the writing is regarded as a matter of considerable importance for credibility and authenticity (see the Book of Daniel). No such concerns are evident in this book, simply because it presents so few clues itself as to when it was written.

Suggestions for the date of the book range widely. Evangelical scholars who have produced standard introductions to the Old Testament books have found no consensus. Gleason L. Archer argues for a date of about 830 B.C., during the minority of King Joash. Roland K. Harrison settles for a date somewhere before 400 B.C., during the period of the restoration. More recently, a date near 600 B.C. has been presented by the critical scholars E. Konig and A. S. Kapelrud. The recent introduction by the Fuller Seminary team of William La Sor, David Hubbard, and Frederic Bush accepts this middle-ground date. It is also my choice, stated with the caution the facts in this case must warrant.

The Prophet's Message

The argument based on the concept of the Day of Yahweh is the most impressive. This is the principal theological contribution of the Book of Joel. It is also Zephaniah's major concern, whose book is dated internally to begin in 627 B.C. While still debated, it seems likely that Joel wrote near the time of Zephaniah. When we compare the way in which these two writers speak of the Day of Yahweh, it is hard to imagine centuries separating their writings. See again a comparison of Zephaniah 1:14–16 and Joel 2:2 (cf., Joel 1:15; 2:11). The date of c. 600 B.C. is frightfully near the destruction of the city of Jerusalem (587/586 B.C.), a factor which adds poignancy to Joel's message.

Without any outside corroboration of the year of the terrible locust invasion, we may suggest that Joel ministered in Jerusalem about twenty years following the calls of Zephaniah and Jeremiah. If our reconstruction is correct, the prophet Joel would have lived in the frantic last years of the kingdom of Judah. Perhaps the king at the time of his preaching was Jehoiakim (608-597 B.C.).

The end was at hand, but so was a new beginning.

For Further Study

1. Read Jeremiah 1–3 to see how this prophet relates the events of his life to the narrative and message of his book.

2. Compare and contrast the first verse of two of each of the writing prophets with the opening words of Joel. Look for what is said about the prophet and what is said respecting his reception of the word of God.

3. Read the introduction—especially the section on the date and setting—to the Book of Joel in two Bible dictionaries, and observe varied positions. How comfortable are you with the position advanced in this book? Can you summarize the problem of the dating and setting of the Book of Joel?

Chapter 3

Calamity!
(Joel 1:1–12)

Bad News

The old bromide "No news is good news" seems particularly apt in our day when so much of what is news seems to be so very bad. As I write these words, the newscasts and printed media have no shortage of evil things to describe. I suspect that as you read these words, stories of evil happenings are still sufficient to ruin your news day as well.

One tragi-comic scene in an outtake from a popular film presents a happy fellow walking down the main street of his small town. He plugs a quarter in a newspaper stand, takes out the paper, and gazes in horror at the headline. The fellow rushes back to the stand, plugs in another quarter, and stuffs the paper back into the stand. Then we see him resuming his happy walk down the street.

The scene is hilarious because it strikes so close to where many people live. It is just that we rarely do as this comic does. We continue to read the news and to grieve at the troubles that seem so often to pounce upon us in our world.

Troubles are not new, nor is bad news an invention of our day. We just have better means available to spread the bad news more quickly to more people. Ancient cuneiform inscriptions on clay texts are no match for modern telecommunications.

There has always been trouble in the world, ever since our first parents brought calamity and ruin to the race when they betrayed God's trust.

25

Unprecedented Plague

There was a great deal of trouble in the days of Joel. In the opening salvo of his book there was an unprecedented national calamity caused by an horrific plague of locusts. The insects had come in such numbers, one assault following another in four sickening rotations, that the agriculture of the nation was thoroughly destroyed. Here was a trouble that affected all the people.

Joel begins his message with an appeal to the nation, first to the elders, then to the people of the land.

> Hear this, you elders;
> listen, all who live in the land (1:2, first half).

The Hebrew verbs translated "hear" and "listen" form a common pairing in the poetic and prophetic literature of the Bible. The first word is the common word meaning "to hear." The second is a verb developed from the noun "ear" and might be rendered more roughly as "use your ears." How very often the teachers in Scripture urge people who have ears to use them to hear the word of the Lord! The great prophet Isaiah begins his book with precisely the same two verbs, but his addressees are the heavens and the earth (see Isa. 1:2).

Joel addresses the elders, the rulers and leaders, as well as the common people ("all who live in the land"). By tying together those two broad, disparate groups, the prophet is making an inclusive call. We call this use of polarities to describe totally a *merism*. A merism is a standard Hebrew literary device that uses opposite particulars but intends for us to include everything in general that falls between those two sets of particulars.

Examples of merism include "heaven and earth" in Genesis 1:1, where God is the creator of the universe. Isaiah also describes the nation Judah in the image of a man who has been beaten to a bloodied pulp, "from the sole of your foot to the top of your head," (1:6) that is, the entire body. Joel uses the merism of "elders and all who live in the land" again in 1:14. In both cases he is addressing the whole of the nation, from the various exalted leaders to the simplest of the common people.

Joel's initial challenge is for the people of the nation to

consider the magnitude of the present national disaster. He uses the rhetorical device of hyperbole, a deliberate exaggeration for effect, by stating that there has never been a disaster comparable to this one they currently experienced. He blends hyperbole with rhetorical question, a question that does not call for an answer, except obvious assent.

> Has anything like this ever happened in your days
> or in the days of your forefathers?
> Tell it to your children,
> and let your children tell it to their children,
> and their children to the next generation (1:2–3).

The reason we describe Joel's language here as hyperbolic is that there have in fact been worse things in the memory of the race than the present experience, no matter how very bad this was. Surely, the great flood of Genesis 6–9 was a greater devastation. Certainly, the judgment of God on Sodom and the cities of the plain was more awful. Assuredly, the devastating plagues on the peoples of Egypt by which Yahweh wrested his nascent people from the deathgrip of Pharaoh were more varied and their cumulative power more overwhelming.

But the prophet is able to say at least in recent memory there had never been a plague of insects so very terrible as this one. For those of us who wish to pin down the date of the prophet Joel, we may be disappointed to learn that we do not have any other record of this catastrophe extant.

But it was bad, very bad indeed!

Generation to Generation

Joel says that one generation should transmit the news to the next; that generation, to other children yet unborn.

There are some bad things we wish to forget, if we are able, but some things are so bad they should not be forgotten. Elie Wiesel, the Nobel prize winning author and survivor of the concentration camps in Nazi Europe, believes the Holocaust is one of those terrible things that must not be forgotten. For the danger in forgetting is that the evil might be repeated.

In the case of the plague of locusts, the devastation was so overwhelming that a part of the coping process will be in the expectation that generations to come will look back in sympathy on the peoples who lived through it. Those in our own day who lived through the Great Depression or who survived the Dust Bowl often do not want their experiences to be forgotten either. Younger people should learn from the difficulties of earlier generations to appreciate the peace and prosperity of their own day.

Wave After Wave

The locusts are described in verse 4 in four waves: what green things one wave left, the next would get. What the second wave of locusts managed not to eat, the third would get. And if there were anything at all still green that the third wave of insects missed, such was the precious fodder for the ravenously hungry fourth wave.

The Hebrew words for these four waves of locusts are subject to dispute. Here are some ways that translators have rendered these four words.

KJV	NKJV	NIV
palmerworm	chewing locust	locust swarm
locust	swarming locust	great locusts
cankerworm	crawling locust	young locusts
caterpillar	consuming locust	other locusts

Doubtless you have other translations to compare. There are numerous types of locusts in the world, as well as several stages of development among each of the locusts. It is my impression that the poet chose four handy Hebrew words for locusts, not for entomological specification and exactitude, but to convey an impression of overwhelming devastation. The (as-yet elusive) precise identification of the meaning of these four Hebrew words is not nearly so important as the way the prophet uses these words to pile them one upon another in successive sweeps of all-consuming appetite.

Bad News for Drunks

There is something almost comic about Joel's call to drunkards to awaken from their stupors so that they may weep at the loss of this year's vineyard crops. No grapes today means no wine tomorrow (1:5). But if there is anything humorous in this, it is a bitter, sardonic humor—a gallows humor. The reason for the drunks to get sober enough to feel pain is that there will be no more wine to come to shield them next season from the nastiness of life. A disapproving temperance speaker might say, "It serves them right!"

But Joel's nearly comic words are deadly serious, terribly in earnest. He grips our attention by his appeal to the town drunks, although it is really the leaders and the citizenry whom he has in mind. The call to drunks is a ruse to get the others to pay attention to the seriousness of the situation.

Certainly, this text should not be used as a condemnation of the use of wine. For the next group of people who will suffer from the cutting off of viticulture will be the priests who minister in the temple of God. They will not have wine to use in their divinely-sanctioned libation offerings (1:9).

Indeed, again we have an example of merism. There will be no wine for anyone, not for drunken sots, who waste their lives away in blind, mindless excess; not for the priests of God, who use wine in divine worship; not for anyone else either.

The locust plague of Joel's day had been so thorough in its swath of orgiastic consumption that nothing is left that is green, nothing is left that has leaves, nothing is left that has bark— hardly anything growing in the fields is left at all.

Joel writes,

> A nation has invaded my land,
>   powerful and without number;
> it has the teeth of a lion,
>   the fangs of a lioness (1:6).

Slowly Joel will move from the locust plague of his day to something even more horrible in a future time. He begins this transition of thought by describing the locusts in verse 6 as "a nation," employing the Hebrew term *gôy*, which is usually used to speak of a (human) national entity. The locusts were like a (human) nation in their campaign of conquest. This insect "nation" was powerful and innumerable, its ravenous teeth compared to lions' teeth shredding their prey. But in this case, Joel says, the prey of this alien nation was "my land."

By the personal pronoun in the phrase "my land," we learn that the prophet is not distant or aloof in these events. He also speaks of "my vines" and "my fig trees" (1:7). It was "his" land that was under attack; he, too, was one who suffered. His land was devastated, so the ruin to fields and orchards was a ruin that affected his life. Since the speaker in this first part of the book is the prophet Joel himself, it seems best to understand the pronoun "my" to be his own vantage point. At the same time, the prophet mirrors in this regard the feelings of God himself. For ultimately the land and all the produce are his (see Ps. 24:1).

Jeremiah describes the situation neatly in his parable of Yahweh's love affair with Israel (Jer. 2). Yahweh gave the gift of the land to his people as his bridal gift (see v. 3–7a), but the people had defiled the land by their infidelities. But the land was still the Lord's (v. 7). He had given it to them to use, not to abuse. Their abuse of the land was an assault on his person and an attack on his inheritance.

So the prophet Joel speaks of the land much as God would when he speaks of vineyards and fig trees, of pomegranates and apples (1:12). It is "my land" that he sees suffering, and he shares in the suffering with all the others, just as God suffers at the assault on his land.

Mourning Priests, Despairing Farmers

It is not just drunks who must mourn the loss of the life of the land. So must the priests (1:8–10); assuredly, so must the farmers (1:11–12).

Joel's call for the priests to mourn is introduced by a picture of disconsolate sadness.

> Mourn like a virgin in sackcloth
> grieving for the husband of her youth (1:8).

Imagine a young woman who has come to the cherished hope of her wedding day, only to find that her beloved bridegroom had died the night before. Instead of the lovely gown she had planned to wear, her eyes all a-dance with the sparkle only a bride is able to radiate, her expectations of joy are fully destroyed. In exquisite agony she shreds her gown; in anguish of despair, she rips at her hair. Her face ages in moments. Instead of the soft and delicate fabrics of her erstwhile wedding day, she slowly, sadly pulls on the rough textures of sackcloth. Widowed before she was married, she will never have the same life.

Likewise the priests are to mourn. But their mourning is for a reason even more significant than the disconsolate bride-widow's. They mourn their inability to bring the pleasing sacrifices of grain and drink offerings to Yahweh in the celebrative worship at the holy temple.

Today, when many think of sacrifice in the Old Testament period, they think exclusively of animal sacrifice—the bringing of sheep, bulls, and goats to the bloodied altars of the Lord. In fact, the true worship of God included the sacrifice of varied farm products, such as grains, olive oil, and wines (see Lev. 2; 6:14–23; 7:11–15) because these were the principal products of the Canaanite land where God had brought his people in great joy (Deut. 7:13). The bringing of grains, oil, and wine in sacrifice to God was an expression of gratitude for God's goodness in giving them the gift of the land.

But now there was nothing left to sacrifice. The agriculture of the land was destroyed—no grain, no oil, no wine for the worship of God. So the priests join the drunks in lamenting the famine occasioned by the unprecedented onslaught of locusts.

Here again is the assessment of the prophet.

> The fields are ruined,
> the ground is dried up;
> the grain is destroyed,
> the new wine is dried up,
> the oil fails (1:10).

"The ground is dried up" uses a different verb than the verb "dried up" that describes the new wine in this same verse. Notice that the marginal reading is, "the ground mourns." The problem concerns the Hebrew verb 'ābal. Past authorities present one verb with the meaning, "to mourn"; some newer authorities, impressed particularly by the frequency of the parallel term in various passages translated "withers" (see Isa.

24:4; Jer. 12:4; 23:10), present a homonym for this verb '*āḇal*
meaning "to dry up." That is, "dries up" is regarded as a more
appropriate parallel pair with "withers," than the meaning
"mourns."

The Hebrew verb '*āḇal*, "to mourn," however, is used
figuratively for the lament of inanimate objects, such as gates
(Isa. 3:26). Furthermore, even in the NIV this verb is translated
in the text as "mourns" when the subject is the word "land" (see
Isa. 33:9; Hos. 4:3; Jer. 4:28). My own view is that the
translation "mourns" is preferable in Joel 1:10 as well. Not only
are drunks and priests mourning the loss of agriculture. So, in a
sense, is the very land itself. The language is not unlike that of
the apostle Paul describing the present groaning of creation (see
Rom. 8:22).

And so mourn the farmers as well (1:11). Farmers and vine
growers are to despair and howl in pain as one grieving the
death of a loved one, for the land, dearly loved, is dead of fruit.
Notice the cumulative verbs of distress: "Despair!" "Wail!"
"Grieve!" The harvest in all of its variety is destroyed. Vines are
dried, figs have withered, fruit trees of various descriptions are
all dried up. And so is joy. Here is the saddest note:

> Surely the joy of mankind
> is withered away (1:12, last couplet).

The term translated "joy" is a lovely, expressive word
associated with the Lord's joy at the creation of the universe,
especially the fashioning of the earth as the platform for the
lives of mankind. Lady Wisdom, the marvelous personification
in Proverbs, is pictured as frolicking with joy at the creation of
the world and its habitation by man (Prov. 8:30–31). But now
the joy is gone, gone with the locusts and their ravenous wake.

It is with this sadness that this first segment of the Book of
Joel ends. Those awful plant-eating orthopterous insects in their
leaping and flying migrations have stripped vegetation, it seems,
from the very earth.

And everybody weeps—drunks, priests, farmers, and the
land itself.

For Further Study

1. You may wish to test the assertions of "bad news" in this chapter by thinking through some issues of bad news in the press this week.

2. The poets of the Bible use numerous rhetorical patterns such as hyperbole and merism. Can you identify examples of these patterns of speech in common use today?

3. How does the use of rhetorical devices in language affect your understanding of the inerrancy (trustworthiness, and lack of error) of the Bible? That is, the biblical teaching concerning itself is that the Bible is without error. Does rhetoric threaten this assertion? Relate your general view to the specific instances of the four words for "locust" as described in this chapter.

4. Scripture has much to say about the evils of drunkenness; it also speaks from time to time on the blessings associated with wine. Use a Bible concordance to find some examples of each of these types of texts.

5. The poets of the Bible are drawn regularly to the image of bride and groom for descriptions of happiness. (And to the image of a broken marriage for sadness.) Again, use a Bible concordance to locate other texts similar to Joel's in 1:8.

Sidebar -
P.35 ... Some Commentary
P.36 B's dy
P.37
P.40

Chapter 4

A Time for Fasting and Prayer
(Joel 1:13–20)

Joel and Calamity

Joel the prophet, as we expect, shares many of the preaching emphases of the other prophets of Israel and Judah. He speaks against sin and wickedness, particularly in high places. He calls for repentance and renewal; he warns of coming judgment. Finally he pictures the promises of God for a future day of fulfillment and joy in the presence of Yahweh. With all the prophets, he exults in the wonders of the Lord—both his power in judgment and his mercy in grace.

But beyond these major teaching emphases, the Book of Joel is remarkable in the theology of natural calamity it presents. The message of the book depends upon the invasion of the locusts, which was described in Joel 1:2–12.

Some commentators have tried to allegorize these insects as representative of successive military invasions against Judah. This approach views the locusts as symbols of various nations who came one after the other in a pell-mell frenzy of destruction. But those who take this view do not seem convincing. They lack both specific clues to the identity of the four nations who would have to be involved, as well as textual warrant for moving from insects to military invaders in chapter 1 of Joel.

Other commentators have seen these locusts as some highly symbolic creatures of apocalyptic doom, much like the figurative locusts in the Book of Revelation (Rev. 9:1–11). Again, this approach does not seem to be convincing. It is more likely that

John remembered the locusts of Joel 1 and used that term to describe the fabulous figures he saw in his apocalyptic vision, rather than to presume that Joel saw the same fabulous figures John saw hundreds of years later. There is no warrant to read Revelation 9 back into Joel 1; there is good reason to see a development of imagery from Joel 1 to Revelation 9.

The context of the Book of Joel and the plain literary style of his text suggest that we err if we see the locusts in chapter 1 in any but a literal form. Here was an insect plague that destroyed all agriculture in the land. To spiritualize these locusts as enemy armies, or to mysticise them as apocalyptic beasts, is to lose the poignancy of the text where Joel speaks of drunks, priests, farmers, and the land mourning their losses. The first chapter of Joel is quite literal in meaning; the figurative aspects come a bit later. But there is still more to these locusts than first meets the eye.

Ultimately, Joel will identify these insects as an army of Yahweh (Joel 2:25). By calling the locusts an army, Joel is not presenting them as Babylonians or Syrians, nor as the nightmare creatures a Hieronymus Bosch might have painted from the Book of Revelation. They are still insects, but they are an army sent by God. In this insight, Joel opens a new awareness for us in interpreting what are often called for legal reasons "acts of God."

One of the major lessons from the Book of Joel is that the Lord may use natural phenomena to stir in his people a renewed awareness of his will and ways, a need for repentance and remorse, and a preparation for the coming judgment that will precede the coming of God's kingdom. In biblical thought there is very little room for what we call "nature," even less for "Mother Nature." The biblical viewpoint is of creation and Creator rather than nature and her mother.

Those who pointed to the eruption of Mount St. Helens as the roar of the Lord may have erred in excess. But there may be a sense in which they were right. Any traumatic event of nature/creation, be it flood, fire, eruption, or quake, should call the sensitive ear to listen again to the words of the Lord. A given natural disaster is not a specific indicator of the timing of the future work of the Lord. But the people of God ought to think of

every natural calamity as Joel described the locusts of his day—
a marker that the Day of Yahweh is at hand (Joel 1:15). This is
the central issue of this chapter. It is an issue that besets us often
in our own lives and calls for our discussion.

Volcanoes and the Wrath of God

Perhaps one hundred thousand people in the high Andes
Mountains have died in my lifetime due to the violent up-
heavals of earth, flows of lava, clouds of steam and gases, and
engulfing mudfalls associated with the volcanoes that belch and
fume. I confess that usually I am nearly oblivious to these
peoples and their sufferings, since they are so distant from my
own home and so far from my experience. They live in another
hemisphere, on another continent; they might as well be on
another planet.

Then a volcano erupted nearly in my own backyard.
Finally, I began to think of the frightful lives of those who live
on the slopes of other seething mountains so far away from me.
For the first time in my experience I gave thought to what it is
like to live where supposedly dormant volcanoes are apt to
rouse themselves again.

On 18 May 1980, the Sunday of the first eruption of Mount
St. Helens in Washington State, I was preaching in a church in a
suburb of Portland, Oregon. I had chosen a prophetic theme that
included the topic of the coming wrath of God that would
precede the establishment of the kingdom of our Savior, the
Lord Jesus Christ. My text was Psalm 97. Verse 5 reads, "The
mountains melt like wax before Yahweh." Shortly before the
second service began, a woman, one of my seminary students,
rushed to me and said with great animation, "Dr. Allen! What
you said about the mountains melting like wax? It is happening,
right now; St. Helens is erupting!"

In the weeks that followed that violent phase of the
mountain, some preachers presented messages to the effect that
Mount St. Helens blew because of the anger of God against the
people of the Northwest. Without any desire to cover over the
serious and sordid sins of the people of our region, some pastors
in our area suggested that if it were truly the wrath of God that
provoked the mountain to blow, they could think of a lot of

places more deserving of God's anger than a small region of southwestern Washington. Some had their fingers pointed south, about a thousand miles south!

But there were other ideas about the role of God's hand in this eruption. The Jews for Jesus missionaries had used creative tracts called "Broadsides" in their ministry for several years. These are untraditional in format and in content, but they each point to the necessity for a confrontation with the person and work of God in one's life, with the need for the individual to come to know the Savior, Y'shua, Jesus.

The Jews for Jesus Broadside issued in the wake of the Mount St. Helens' eruption said that this mountain had not erupted because God was angry. It had erupted because it is a volcano, and volcanoes are supposed to erupt when the conditions are right for the eruptive phase. This is how God made volcanoes to behave.

Then the tract went on to say that there is something more to erupting volcanoes or quaking earth. These events are portents. Ultimately they point to coming judgment.

I would also suggest that the eruption of volcanoes, the quaking of the earth's moving plates, the flooding of rivers, the violent storms that uproot trees and overwhelm cities are also portents. They are portents of the judgment of God that will one day visit this earth.

As volcanoes, so locusts—both may alert people to reality in God.

Locusts and God's Wrath

The incursion of the locusts brings many people today to wonder, Was this just a natural phenomenon? Was this simply something inherent in locusts, and this just happened to be a very bad year? Or was this locust invasion the work of God in the judgment of his people? Was this a natural disaster? Or was this a supernatural visitation?

How are believers to interpret the violent intrusions of the elements of God's creation that bring upheaval to the earth, distress and death to countless people, and ruination to the vegetation and fauna of a region? Are these the random zapping activities of God in his pique? Are they his calculated judgments? Are they just nature doing its thing? Or are they something else again?

Whenever a cataclysmic event takes place, thoughtful, believing people will ask questions.

- They will ask if this event might not be the judgment of God, for surely he has used the elements of his creation to vent his wrath in times past, and he will use the elements of creation in his wrath in the future. We should not presume that he could not do this very thing in our time.

- They will ask if a particular disaster might not also just be something God has allowed his creation to do, based upon the way things are. For it is the nature of engorged rivers to flood, of violently moving plates to quake, of super-heated magma to erupt. When we assert with the psalmist that the earth and all that is in it belong to the Lord (Ps. 24:1), we include the phenomena and the processes God has invested into his world—they are all under his control.

- They will also ask what they may learn from the disaster that is suggestive of the coming day of the wrath of God on the earth as a whole. For that day of wrath will come and will transcend all other experiences of man in tumult.

The Book of Joel may teach us to view so-called "natural disasters" as divine portents of judgment to come. Joel does not actually state in this first chapter that the invasion of locusts was a direct visitation of God's wrath upon his people. He withholds that identification until later in his book (see 2:25). However, Joel certainly does present the disaster as a portent of the coming Day of Yahweh (1:15).

Every terrible disaster may be viewed by the believing community as God's sovereign allowance for his creation in the violence and upheaval of the post-Fall world. And every such disaster may also be regarded as a portent, a foreboding warning: The day of the overwhelming judgment of God is soon to come. These events are the creation's aerobics for the grand judgment, for the Day of Yahweh.

A Time to Lament

Hence, the prophet Joel calls to the priests and the temple ministers to adopt the physical pose of mourning for their losses, remorse for their sins. He asks them to proclaim a holy fast, a sacred assembly for the nation, to beseech the mercy of Yahweh in the midst of this terrible disaster (1:13–14).

The lament over the destruction of agriculture is particularly hard for the priests because of the lack of materials to be used in the sacrifice of pleasant grace. Let's not underestimate the importance of presenting sacrifices in the temple. These were the means whereby the fate of the nation would be protected, the good of the people preserved, and the glory of God magnified. Consequently, cutting off goods for temple worship was a major issue, a life-and-death issue, not exaggerated words of lament. To lose the elements of sacrifice was in some way to lose touch with God himself. For these reasons, the prophet speaks so clearly: Call them to the house of Yahweh and there let them cry out to Yahweh (1:14). Perhaps another day will bring his answer of hope for a starving, draught-stricken people.

Underlying Joel's words is the presumption that the people are in a state of sin and need very much to repent, to express remorse, and to seek the mercy of God in the face of this calamity. For any day of calamity is suggestive of the dreadful day to come.

The Dreadful Day

It is in Joel 1:15 that we first confront the concept of the Day of Yahweh:

> Alas for that day!
>   For the day of Yahweh is near;
>   it will come like a destruction from the Almighty.

This verse is potent. It is anticipative of the larger section in Joel 2:1–11 describing the coming Day of Yahweh. But here we have just one verse. Its juxtaposition with the calamity of the locusts gives us the notion of portent. Joel does not say that the locust invasion was the Day of Yahweh. He does say that the

Day of Yahweh will come with the same suddenness and destructiveness as the locust invasion.

The NIV translation of the first colon of verses 15 is, "Alas for that day." This is an expressive, culturally sensitive rendering of the Hebrew phrasing, "Alas the day!" The Hebrew word describing this day is *'ahāh*. This word is onomatopoetic; that is, the sound describes its meaning. As the word "buzz" is explained by its own sound, so the world *'ahāh* is meaning enough. It is a word of painful anguish, an expiration of air as one has a blow to the abdomen, a grunt of pain when hurt deeply. Such is the response to the coming of the Day of Yahweh: *'ahāh!*

Two further things are said about this day. First, its nearness: it is soon to come. Second, its nature is that it comes as a destruction from the Almighty. The nearness of the Day of Yahweh is a constant in the eschatological future. It is not to be regarded as distant, as remote; it is near us, upon us, just beside us—the beep of a clock away.

The word "near" in Hebrew presents the Day as ominous, almost as though this day were hovering nearby, ready to make its move on the calendar of man from the schedule of God.

The nature of the day is expressed by the phrase, "like destruction from the Almighty." In the Hebrew text, there is a verbal play on words in this phrasing. The term *shōd*, "destruction," and the name for God, *shaddai*, "the Almighty," have a very similar sound. The name for God that is translated in the NIV as "the Almighty" is the important, but difficult to translate Hebrew word *Shaddai*.

Because of the similarity in sound between this name of God and the verb "to destroy," some have thought that the name of God, *Shaddai*, is a term suggesting overwhelming destruction. Actually, this name for God appears to be a word that expresses the majestic height and enduring glory of God, in whose presence there are demands of blameless walk (see Gen. 17:1), as well as a protective place of shelter from the storms and stresses of life (see Ps. 91:1–2).

In verses 16–18 the prophet restates the effects of the calamity on the agriculture of Judah. Food that was growing on the fields and orchards had been stripped away, as it were, in front of their very eyes. The loss of food is also a loss of joy for the person in his own life, and especially for the believer in his worship of God.

The covenant that God established with Israel through Moses has repeated emphases on the productivity of the land that was enjoyed when Israel was faithful to her God (see Deut. 8:6–9). When the people would see the harvests and enjoy their plenty, then they were to give God praise for the good land which was his gift to them (Deut. 8:10). A failure to give praise to God, and to live out his commands in life, would turn their plenty into poverty, God's grace into wrath.

The association of harvest and worship was inevitable; it was God's plan. To worship God was a happy task because worship was associated with the wholeness of life.

With the crops destroyed and the fields ruined, there was no joy nor gaiety in the temple. All was in ruin. From seeds to storehouses, from granaries to the grain itself, all was gone.

The prophet moves from the joylessness in the temple to the moaning and milling about of the cattle (v. 18). For they, too, suffer. Pastures are destroyed, the herds and the flocks are suffering along with man.

The Prophet's Prayer

Perhaps the most touching note in the Book of Joel is his prayer in Joel 1:19–20. As an angered prophet of the Almighty God, Joel might have looked at the sinning populace of Jerusalem and Judah with disdain. He might have thought they received what they deserved. He might have looked at the suffering animals and said that it was too bad that they had to join man in suffering, but that was the way things worked out sometimes. He might have set himself apart from his people and their misery, but he does not do any of these things.

Joel is a part of the community. He, too, faces hunger and anguish. The locusts have destroyed the food for the just and the unjust. His basic humanity is touched by the suffering of the animals of the fields. Joel is real, a genuine person, who senses with his people, suffers with them, prays with them.

Joel prays in these two verses a poignant, lamentive prayer of a desparately hurting believer, pleading with his God for help from distress. He prays directly to Yahweh for deliverance, as he describes the parched fields, the bare trees, the panting animals and the dry stream beds.

Here is a prophet who not only pronounces the word of God. Here is one who also interacts with God on behalf of his people and his land. Here the prophet has become a priest, interceding with God on behalf of others, as well as for himself.

When Joel calls for a time of fasting and prayer, he joins in these disciplines of worship to the great Yahweh.

For Further Study

1. Are there other portions of the Bible that develop a "theology of natural calamity" as Joel does? What might these be?

2. You may have access to a commentary that allegorizes or spiritualizes the insects of Joel 1:4–7. How is this done? Is it convincing?

3. This chapter presents a point of view toward natural calamities and portents of coming judgment. How does this differ from saying these calamities *are* God's judgment? What is your reaction to these points of view?

4. Compare the prayer of Joel in 1:19-20 to the anguish of Jeremiah (Jer. 9:1-2), and then to the command of God for Jeremiah not to pray for his people any longer (Jer. 14:11–18).

Chapter 5

The Day of Yahweh
(Joel 2:1–11)

New Perspectives

The issues of the Book of Joel really begin in the second chapter. Joel is not just a book about destructive insects, no matter how numerous, nor simply about agricultural failure, no matter how grievous. The Book of Joel is principally concerned with the necessary work of God in the impending judgment of his people's many sins. It is also very much concerned with the determination of God to bring to pass the ultimate fulfillment of his great promises for future blessing and deliverance. That is, Joel fits in squarely with the grand tradition of prophetism in Israel. He presents a message of judgment and a promise of blessing. The message of judgment that Joel presents is truly fearful; the message of God's grace and blessing will be equally awesome.

The second chapter of Joel is markedly different from the first chapter. Several elements account for these differences. First, there is a new speaker. The speaker in chapter 1 was Joel the prophet, who speaks of God to the people and to God in prayer on behalf of the people. The speaker in chapter 2 is the Lord himself. Note, for example, the pronoun in verse one: "in Zion . . . my holy hill." This is the language of God. So is the special phrasing of verse 12, "declares Yahweh."

To say the new speaker is Yahweh is not to forget the material presented in the introductory chapter on the ways in which the prophets speak the word of God. The prophets are not mechanical dictation machines God uses as transmitting devices. The prophets are always vital persons who take the word of God, which they receive in some mysterious manner, and then give that word shape through their own personality, means of expression, and artistic intent.

One of the ways that a prophet might give expression to the words of God is to present that word in the third person, more from the prophet's own stance as a man of this world. This is Joel's method in chapter 1 where the prophet is the speaker. Another way is to present that word in the first person, more directly from the stance and perspective of heaven. In this way God is presented as the speaker in chapter 2. In either case, the basic message comes from God. The expression of that message is through the art and style of the prophet, with the Spirit of God working throughout the entire procedure to assure the integrity of the resultant proclamation.

Second, there is a different tone in these chapters. Chapter 1 has a tone of lament and despair provoked by the ruinous national agricultural disaster. Chapter 2 presents a tone of alarm and fear, anticipative of a more terrible day to come. Actually, the locust invasion is just a preparatory, conditioning event. The prophet moves from a restricted, local devastation of his own day to a world-wide catastrophe in the future. *Probably more toward destruction of Jerusalem AD 70*

Third, and related to these others, there is a difference in the time period of the chapters. The time period of the first chapter is the current scene in the life of the prophet Joel. The time period of the second is a more distant day in the future, the great and terrible Day of Yahweh.

But not all things are different in these chapters. There remains a dynamic thematic flow and development of ideas. Some significant words in the first chapter are put to new uses or are expanded significantly in the second. What are natural locusts in unusual numbers in chapter 1 become very unnatural, fearsome beasts, horrific by their very nature.

Most notably, chapter 2:1–11 describes the coming Day of Yahweh, an expression that has its roots in chapter 1. The first mention of this dreaded day was actually given in Joel 1:15, an anticipation of the coming day of God's wrath based upon the present experience of the people of Jerusalem. This verse in chapter 1 is almost a premonition that something far more significant was to be made of the national disaster than people might realize.

We are accustomed to sing in praise of God for the gift of a day in the words of Psalm 118:24,

> This is the day that Yahweh has made;
> let us rejoice and be glad in it.

Sing

But another day of God's making does not call for praise and rejoicing; this day compels a gasp, a wheeze, a frenzy of alarm. For this reason, as we have noted, Joel 1:15 introduces the concept of the Day of Yahweh with the word *'ahāh*, translated by the NIV, "Alas for that day!" Chapter 2 helps us to see more of the reason for alarm.

The Importance of the Day

The revelation of the Day of Yahweh is particularly associated with the teaching of the prophet Joel, but it was not his message alone. The prophecy of the coming Day of Yahweh is an integral part of Old Testament biblical theology and indeed, of the prophetic message of the New Testament as well. We need not list all texts relating to the coming Day of Yahweh to amplify the teaching of Joel in this brief study. But we may cite two major texts in the Hebrew Bible and two in the New Testament that should be studied along with Joel. These are Isaiah 13:1–13; Zephaniah 1:14–2:3; Matthew 24, especially verses 29–35; Revelation 19:11–21.

Isaiah 13 uses language very similar to Joel 2 in describing the terrible coming Day of Yahweh. Isaiah's prophecy begins as an oracle against Babylon (Isa. 13:1) but soon moves to the same eschatological frame as in Joel 2. So much of Joel's language in 1:15 and 2:1–11 is similar to that of Isaiah 13:1–13 that some relationship is likely. Conventional dating of Isaiah in the late-eighth to early seventh-centuries B.C. leads us to presume that his was the earlier writing and that Joel (whom we have dated at c. 600 B.C.) was dependent upon Isaiah, rather than the reverse. In each case there was the word of Yahweh in the prophet's mouth; however, the prophet Joel may well have also studied and made use of the words of Isaiah to frame his own message.

Compare, for example, Joel 1:15 with Isaiah 13:6; Joel 2:1–2 with Isaiah 13:9; Joel 2:10 with Isaiah 13:10.

The precise time of the ministry of the prophet Joel is in dispute, as was noted earlier. Nevertheless, some modern scholars now argue that Zephaniah and Joel were contemporaries, the approach taken in this book. The strong similarities of language and imagery describing the coming Day of Yahweh in Joel 2:1–11 and Zephaniah 1:14–2:3 seem to be explained best by seeing these two prophets of Yahweh sharing a common vision. At this time, the nation to whom they preached was standing on the brink of its own disaster in the final years before the Babylonian invasion, siege, and destruction of Jerusalem. In any event, one moves quite easily between Joel 2 and Zephaniah 1. Not only is the topic the same, so is much of the language. We will notice also the use of the subject matter of Joel 2, Zephaniah 1, and Isaiah 13 in the teaching of Jesus (Matt. 24) and in the Apocalypse (Rev. 19). But now, on to our text!

Sound the Alarm

The second chapter begins with these words of alarm.

> Blow the trumpet in Zion;
> sound the alarm on my holy hill (2:1).

As is characteristic in this book, the central locus is the city of Jerusalem. "Zion" is a word that is used several ways in the Bible. It begins as a term for the Jebusite city of Jerusalem that was conquered by David (see 2 Sam. 5:7); at times, as a term for the site of the holy temple (see Amos 1:2); or as a term for the whole city of Jerusalem (as in Ps. 48:2); and for the people of the city (as in Mic. 3:10, 12), particularly the godly (Zeph. 3:16).

There is a sardonic note of irony here. The alarm trumpets are to be blown in the city of God not to call his aid, but to warn the people of the judgment that God is about to bring upon them.

These words on trumpets remind us of the instruction on the silver trumpets given in Numbers 10. The trumpets were to be sounded to call the wilderness community into assembly before the Tent of Meeting (Num. 10:3), or, if only one horn sounded, to call the leaders of the clans to assemble (v. 4).

Another tattoo sequence would set the people forward on their march within their families and clans (vv. 6–7).

More important for the understanding of this passage in Joel is the section in Numbers 10 describing the use of trumpets when Israel was to go into battle. The trumpets were to be sounded when Israel went into battle in their own land against an oppressing enemy. The sound of the trumpet was to be regarded as a prayer, a signal to God, who would respond and rescue his people in the battle (v. 9). The trumpets were also to be used at times of rejoicing and sacrifice as a memorial to the Lord (v. 10).

In the Book of Joel the trumpet, specifically the *shôphār*, is to be sounded as an alarm, not because of an advancing army of insolent enemies of God, whom he will sweep away in his wrath as he protects his own. In this case, the enemy is God himself, more particularly by means of the approaching Day of Yahweh (Joel 2:1). A trumpet call will not bring his help; here the call is to warn the people of the awful reality they face.

The Coming of the Day

The potent force in this section is described as "the Day of Yahweh" (or "the Day of the LORD;" see author's foreword). This phrase has brought about considerable controversy. Here is a basic definition: *The Day of Yahweh is that period of time when the Lord dramatically, profoundly, and intimately intervenes in the affairs of men, either for wrath or for restoration and blessing.*

We need to be careful in describing this phrase or we may lead ourselves to some difficulty. For one thing, the nature of the time is not to be regarded as a twenty-four-hour period, as we usually use the term "day," but an extended period of uncertain length. That is, the term "day" confirms that the phrase does relate to time, but this is not by any means a term of mathematical exactitude.

An analogy, which will only be helpful to some, is to think of the "days" of the creative week of Genesis 1. Many readers, of course, believe that these days are twenty-four-hour periods, marked by morning and evening, just as days in our own experience. Others, however, have long argued that the "days" of Genesis are not so much indicators of the length of time for a particular creative action, as they are literary devices to describe various orders of the creative actions of our great God. In either case, the concept of "days" and the creative work of God is not insignificant for the phrase the Day of Yahweh. As Yahweh has had his special "days" in the beginning of his works, so God has his special "day" at the time of the end of his works.

Second, we do not wish to suggest by the definition that there are times when God is not profoundly, intimately, and dramatically related with his people. Still, there are some times when, it seems, God is far more involved in the lives of his people; other times, it seems, God lingers, evaluating from a distance. God is never altogether distant from his people, but there are times when he is more profoundly near than others. These times of his more direct intervention may be described as the Day of Yahweh.

Third, the Day of Yahweh has both negative and positive ramifications. There is a dreadful side to the nature of the Day of Yahweh, which is central in our present text and which will impress us deeply in this section. But there is also a beautiful and blessed side to the Day of Yahweh, as we will see in chapter 3 of Joel.

As we think of "the Day of Yahweh," we should naturally think in terms of God's intimate and profound workings on the earth rather than just as a period of a certain number of hours. The time element is incidental to the phrase as a whole.

The coming of the Great Day is something that calls for trembling and quaking fear. For this day has no precedent and no follow-up. This day is unique in its profound darkness (v. 2a-b). The language of the first bicolon (two part line) of verse 2 uses four different nouns for darkness that the NIV translates "darkness," "gloom," "clouds," and "blackness." These words, like the term "day," force us to recollect Genesis 1. In the beginning of the works of God as described in Genesis 1:2, the whole of primordial matter was enshrouded in darkness, a profound absence of light. The first creative work of God was the bringing into being of light (Gen. 1:3), a call of his word.

The ominous approach of overwhelming darkness in the oracle of Joel may be seen in some way and to some degree as a

NO WAY

return to the Genesis 1:2 state of chaos and ruin. The God who brought forth light was now about to take it away in the judgment of his new, awful day.

The Day is Near

Another aspect of the coming day is the nearness of its approach. The Hebrew text of verse 1d reads "for the Day of Yahweh is coming, surely it is near." One of the great vantage points of the biblical world is a special sense of time that pervades the text. We tend to think in terms of sequential action, of time coming moment by moment. The Day of Yahweh is perceived by the prophet as in some way standing outside our time, yet very soon to irrupt into our sphere.

Time may be seen as more than just linear. There is also a sense in which special times are "near," that is, parallel to, ready to burst in. This is what some Christians mean by their belief in the immanent return of Christ. It is not just that there is a time toward which we are all moving and we will all arrive, but at which the rapture of the church will take place. The immanent view of the return of Jesus Christ means that there is another sphere of time altogether different from our own that is parallel to, near to, and alongside our sense of time. This may be a part of the mystery of the words of Jesus in Matthew 24:36, "No one knows about that day or hour." At any moment, from our perspective, that other sphere may burst into ours and "the time" will have come.

So the time of the Day of Yahweh is near; it is approaching. It is more than a red-letter day on a calendar or a circled number in a date book. It is an existing reality that is parallel to our own time and may burst into our sphere at any moment—the moment of God's pleasure. The Day of Yahweh is not self-existing, of course. It has no mind of its own. It will not irrupt into our world willy-nilly. But, under the hand of God, it remains ready, dynamic, nearly-present. Boldly it approaches; soon it draws near.

The Army of That Day

Yet another element in the coming Day of Yahweh is the sense of impending doom it presents in the approach of a vast,

terrible army. Joel compares the coming of this army to the
gradual spreading of the reddish light of dawn across the
mountains (2:2c), ordinarily a source of joy, but here one of
terror because this is a day of wrath. For what is spreading
across the mountains like the dawn is a vast and mighty army,
unprecedented and unmatched later.

This army is invincible; its path of march, a swath of
devastation. Here is Sherman's march through Georgia magnified many times. As the ghastly army approaches, all before it
is ignited into flame; behind it, all is blazing. Before the army
the land is comparable to the Garden of Eden; behind it is
nothing but desert, for nothing at all escapes (2:3). In such a
vivid contrast, the prophet speaks of a primordial paradise
turned into a desert wasteland—what an overwhelming sense of
destruction.

Joel 2:4–5 describe the appearance of this army. In the
warfare of Joel's day, where most soldiers were on foot, the
mounted soldier and the charioteer were like rockets and tanks.
Joel uses the most impressive imagery of terrible warfare in his
own experience to describe the sheer power and dread of this
coming army. He compares them to horses and to chariots, and
he describes them in ways to assault our senses. We hear their
noise, and the crackling of their fires. We see them leaping and
galloping. We smell the fire. We smell our own fear.

We also understand the fear of the nations (Joel 2:6). The
NIV translation, "nations are in anguish," represents a Hebrew
phraseology that speaks of quaking, violent fear. The same word
speaks of a woman experiencing difficult childbirth, wrenching
with contortion and the all-embracing pains of her contractions.
Here the contractions are not from the process of delivery of a
child, but the contractions of an all-engulfing terror. The second
colon of verse 6 speaks of every face turning pale. The Hebrew
term here is found elsewhere only in Nahum 2:10. The meaning
is somewhat problematic. Literally, it seems to mean "gathering
of heat" and would indicate a reddened face from fear, anger, or
agitation. Whether the faces of the nations are flushed in anger
(compare the wording of Isa. 13:8, "their faces aflame") or
"drained of all color" (Joel 2:6b, NKJV), the result is the same—a
physically terrifying, body-gripping sense of horror.

The Language of the Prophet

As readers, we have to ask what type of language this is. Is Joel describing something very literal or very spiritual? Or is he describing something that is literal, but with the use of figurative language? Certainly, we understand that his language is somewhat figurative because of his pronounced use of simile. The army is "like dawn" (2:2), their appearance is "like crackling fire" and "like a mighty army" (2:5). The use of these various comparisons is figurative language. Joel describes the army in palpable terms to convey deep impressions.

Figurative language may be used to describe something nonliteral, abstract, and spiritual. The portrait of Lady Wisdom in Proverbs 1–9, for instance, is a special use of language to present an abstraction, "wisdom," in a more palpable form to the reader. Figurative language may also be used to describe something very literal indeed. The sword in the mouth of the conquering Jesus in Revelation 19:15 is a figurative expression, but the victims of his wrath will vouch for the reality of the judgment. The type of language does not determine whether something is literal or not. The function of this elevated language is to appeal to our senses, to help us to experience more profoundly the impression Joel desires us to have.

One thing we sense in this section of Joel is the apocalyptic tenor of his writing. It is similar to parts of Daniel and Ezekiel and is in some ways anticipative of parts of the Revelation. The relative late dating we have suggested (see introduction) is in accord with these stylistic features. Joel 2:1–11 is quite similar in use of language to the apocalyptic writers of the Bible. He is describing judgmental scenes in vivid, palpable terms that are an assault to our senses, that leave us worn out in the experience.

The Advance of the Army

Joel 2:7–10 presents the description of the advance of this terrible army against their foes. The army is invincible. They know no barriers, are subject to no blockades. They march with the steady purpose of a victorious army; each man does his job without interfering with his fellow, not even breaking ranks when they plunge through defenses.

They enter the city at will. Walls are no deterrents, nor are buildings. Windows are their entryway. They surge and pulse and make their way in.

They are like locusts! Who can build a wall to keep out locusts? This invading army has its way just as the locusts did in the experience of the people described in chapter 1.

And their sway is felt in the heavens. Joel writes in mind-boggling terms.

> Before them the earth shakes,
>   the sky trembles,
> the sun and moon are darkened,
>   and the stars no longer shine (2:10).

Could be Babylon

This is the language of the *eschaton.*This is the language of final judgment. Here is a prophecy such as in Isaiah 13:10, quoted by Jesus in Matthew 24:29. This is the language of Isaiah 24, especially verse 4. This is out of the scenario of the Battle of Armageddon, of the final battle, of the last days. Joel has moved from the natural locusts to the invincible power of the supernatural armies of God who will destroy all foes and initiate the kingdom of the Promised One. One who reads Joel 2 is driven naturally to the words of John in Revelation 19:11–21. One is also reminded sharply of the words of Jesus in his sermon on the Mount of Olives, especially Matthew 24:29–30. The modern reader of Joel 2 senses the power of these words, and their relevance, even more deeply than we may presume they were felt in the ancient day of Joel's pronouncement. For we are nearer the day.

Yahweh's Day

All of the language of verses 1–10 builds in anticipation for the climactic words of verse 11.

> Yahweh thunders
>   at the head of his army;
> his forces are beyond number,
>   and mighty are those who obey his command.
> The day of Yahweh is great;

it is dreadful.
Who can endure it?

The sound that overwhelms the jostle and bustle of the immense numbers of the invading army is the voice of Yahweh, thundering loudly, roaring boldly. The Hebrew text reads, "So Yahweh gives his voice." The NIV rendering "Yahweh thunders" is appropriate, for the crash of thunder is a vivid association with the thought of the voice of God.

Verse 11 tells us that the invincible, destroying army of verses 2–10 is not an army of the wicked, but of the righteous. Here is an army not of the evil one, but of Yahweh himself. It is he who is at the head of his own army. This is the portrait of the Savior-Warrior John also saw in Revelation 19:11–16. Those who are with him are exceedingly numerous, overwhelmingly powerful, unhesitatingly obedient, and altogether victorious.

There simply is no day to be compared with the Day of Yahweh! It is dreadful. The Hebrew term is *nôrā'*, a form of the verb "to fear," and is modified by the adjective "very." This day is exceedingly awe-provoking, it is "very terrible" (NKJV).

The rhetorical question by which Joel ends this section of his message, "Who can endure it?", is suggestive of the words of Jesus.

"For then there will be great distress, unequaled from the beginning of the world until now—and never to be equaled again. If those days had not been cut short, no one would survive, but for the sake of the elect those days will be shortened" (Matt. 24:21–22).

The teaching of Joel meshes into the teaching of Jesus. It also reflects the teaching of Isaiah.

For Yahweh has a day of vengeance,
    a year of retribution, to uphold Zion's cause.
        (Isa. 34:8).

Our only comfort in such a context is to realize that this does not end the prophetic message. After the worst will come the best; in the midst of fury there is the offer of the mercy of the Lord. This we see in the next chapter.

For Further Study

1. Reread chapters 1 and 2 of Joel and note anew the differences in style, form, and perspective. Note as well some of the connective elements.

2. The "Day of Yahweh" ("day of the LORD") text of Joel 2:1-11 has numerous similarities with Isaiah 13:1-13 and Zephaniah 1:14-2:3. Take a sheet of paper, arrange it sideways, draw two lines to present three columns, and label each "Isaiah 13," "Joel 2," and "Zephaniah 1-2." Note the similarities among these three texts.

3. Use a Bible dictionary and a concordance to develop a study of the biblical use of the word "Zion."

4. Think through the author's definition of "the Day of Yahweh." Then rewrite this definition in your own words, attempting to include the necessary complements of this term.

5. Think through the issues of time as *near*. Can you develop a better, clearer way to state the issue of the dynamic nature of time in this respect?

Chapter 6

The Grace of Yahweh
(Joel 2:12–17)

An Unexpected Mercy

The bitter taste of the issues of Joel 2:1–11 we studied in chapter 5 still clings to our tongues. They are as a few drops of the acrid, mineral-laden water of the Dead Sea, inadvertently touched to the mouth that resists all purifying rinsings. Joel's words of judgment are a shock to our bodies; our ears ring with his words. We are like a group of people who have seen a horror film and will expect troubled dreams because of the unpleasant images that have assaulted our senses. As one intense woman said to me following a message on the coming, final battle, "I don't like that!" Well, she was right. We are not supposed to "like" the message of the judgment of God. He does not "like" it either!

As such, we are scarcely prepared for the sweetness and loveliness of the words of Joel 2:12–17, words that begin,

> "Even now," declares Yahweh,
> "return to me with all your heart,
> with fasting and weeping and mourning."
> Rend your heart
> and not your garments.
> Return to Yahweh your God,
> for he is gracious and compassionate,
> slow to anger and abounding in love,
> and he relents from sending calamity (2:12–13).

Joel 2:1–11 was all fear and bluster; Joel 2:12–17 is all calm and serene. The abruptness of the change of tone, the startling juxtaposition of wrath and mercy, the sudden swing from Yahweh's anger to Yahweh's gentle compassion—these are among the delightful surprises the prophets bring to us, as they did to those who first heard them preach.

Old Testament Wrath

Some people have a negatively skewed understanding of the Bible. They tend to think of the grace of God as an exclusively New Testament preserve, and the wrath of God as the special theme of the Old Testament. They seem to presume that "grace" is a New Testament innovation, that "love" was not a Hebrew word, that the Old Testament is the harshness of Law and the New Testament is the beauty of gospel.

It is not unusual to think so compartmentally about these things. We imagine that the very names "old" and "new," which we commonly use to designate the two Testaments of Scripture, are believed to describe the change from wrath to grace on the part of God.

In fact, there is as much of the wrath of God in the New Testament as there is in the Old, and as much of the grace of God in the Old as there is in the New. The very designation "Old" Testament has become misleading. There is an old covenant, that which God made with Israel through Moses on Mount Sinai. But there really is no "Old" Testament, in the long-standard meaning of the longer, earlier part of the Bible. The New Testament writers do not refer to the earlier writings of Israel as the "Old" Testament. They consistently speak of these books and writings as "Scripture" (see 2 Tim. 3:16), or that which "is written" (see Acts 15:15). For the writers of the New Testament, the earlier writings were the Scriptures of God, which stands forever (Isa. 40:8).

Throughout Scripture there is the revelation of God, of one God revealing himself. God never changes, nor does his revelation progress from the less likable aspects of his person to the more pleasant. There is no modernity in God's grace, no antiquity in his wrath. God has not gone through some personality change in the so-called silent years between the Testaments. Hence, we should expect that in both parts of our Bibles there will be an interplay of the themes of wrath and grace. So there is.

Mercy in the Balances

At the same time, we are not to make a corresponding mistake by suggesting that there are no differences at all between the Testaments. As Dr. Walter Kaiser insists, the Bible is not a flat book. There is a progression of thought, a development of ideas, an unfolding of truth as the opening of a flower in the stages of its life.

The Hebrew prophets are different from the evangelists of the New Testament period. There is a difference in emphasis; this is true. The prophets were ordained by God principally as the ministers of his bad news, his news of coming judgment. They were also given words of his good news of present mercy and coming promise. Proportionately, there is an emphasis on judgment in the prophetic texts. Today's servants of the Lord are ordained to the gospel ministry. That is, they are set aside for the presentation of God's good news. Nevertheless, in any faithful presentation of the good news of God, there is a corresponding presentation of God's bad news. By this I mean, whenever one hears the Good News (the gospel) and rejects it, that person, knowingly or not, is accepting the bad news of God (his wrath) as his due portion.

We have this truth clearly expressed in the central text on the gospel message in the teaching of Jesus (see John 3). After John reports the interaction between the Lord Jesus and the scholar Nicodemus, he presents the basic message of the gospel in the well loved—and justly so!—words of John 3:16. Yet immediately after the words of God's love for the world expressed in the sending of his uniquely begotten Son, there is the judgmental verdict of God on those who reject his great love. These who wickedly spurn grace deserve wrath; they are condemned already for they have not believed the message of the gospel (John 3:17–21).

The general pattern of the New Testament, then, is not only to offer God's good news to needy sinners, but also to affirm his bad news for those who reject the grace and love of God.

The common pattern for the prophets of ancient Israel was

primarily to announce the judgment of God about wickedness and sin, but then to offer God's grace and love to those who would hear, repent, and respond.

The difference in the two Testaments, then, is not one of message but of method. In both the major portions of the Bible, the Hebrew Scriptures and the New Testament, there is a balance between the wrath and judgment of God and his love and mercy. Those who are not aware of the grace of God in Hebrew Scripture are also likely unaware of the terrible judgment passages in the preaching of Jesus and the writings of Paul. Only a selective, biased reading of the Bible can result in these distortions.

Even Now

This section of the Book of Joel (2:12–17) has two subsections to it. The first, Joel 2:12–14, centers on the person and the character of God, who still offers mercy and deliverance to his sinning people. The second, Joel 2:15–17, presents to the people under certain judgment a plan of action that may help them to avert his wrath, "even now."

Joel 2:12–14 begins with the amazing words, "Even now." Those who are familiar with the ways of the prophets will not be as startled by these words as one who is making a first trek down these ancient pathways. It is the way of the prophets to present grace after judgment; it is the way of God.

This grace, however, is still somewhat difficult, in fact nearly incredible, to believe. After the words describing the certain, overwhelming catastrophe announced in Joel 2:1–11, one hardly expects "even now" (2:12).

The suddenness is enhanced by the solemn interjection, "declares Yahweh." The Hebrew phrasing is characteristic of the prophets. The word translated as a verb, "declares," is a frozen particle that more resembles a noun than a verb. This word, nè um, may also be translated as "the solemn declaration of (Yahweh)." It sometimes comes at the beginning, sometimes in the middle, and sometimes at the end of the prophetic recital of the words of God. Its function is to heighten our awareness of the source of the words we read—they are the genuine words of Yahweh.

Verily

As I read the New Testament accounts of the teaching of our
Savior Jesus, I am regularly struck by his use of the words
"truly, truly, I say to you" (see John 6:47, NASB) to introduce his
sayings or to reinforce their startling truth. This repeated Greek
word, translated "verily, verily" in the King James Version, is
the transliteration of the Hebrew word we know as "amen"
(used at the end of prayers). The Hebrew word is based on a root
meaning "to be firm, sure, established," "to be true."

The English expression "verily, verily" or "truly, truly"
sounds redundant. It is, in fact, an Hebraism whereby the
repetition of the word adds emphasis to the phrase, resulting in
a superlative of sorts: "most certainly," or "most assuredly." The
New King James Version translates this phrase, "most assuredly," and the New International Version, "I tell you the truth."

However, we may decide to translate these words, I believe
that, by using the expression, "truly, truly, I say to you," Jesus is
consciously echoing the prophetic recitation of the words of God
in the Old Testament prophets, "the solemn declaration of
Yahweh." The teaching of Jesus is as authoritative as the
teaching of God in Hebrew Scripture. He does not introduce his
words by the phrasing "truly, truly," because he is afraid of
doubt. Rather, this duplicative, emphatic emphasis on the truth
of his word is in line with its authority. When Jesus speaks, it is
the same as when Yahweh speaks.

Return

The commands God gives his erring people present a happy
alliteration in their English translation, "return," "rend," and
"return" (2:12, 13). Judah was on the very brink of disaster.
Jerusalem was about to be destroyed. Well within a generation,
if we have placed the writing of Joel properly, there would come
the devastating hordes of the Babylonian soldiers, who would
set siege to the city and bring the people to starvation once their
food supplies were exhausted. They would break through and
then finally destroy the walls, decimate soldiers, rape women,
kill children, brutalize the remainder, maim and pillage, burn
and ravage—language fails to deal adequately with the ruin
Babylon would bring to Jerusalem and Judah.

Yet the words of God to her on the brink of this sure disaster are, " 'Even now return to me . . . Rend your heart . . . Return to Yahweh,' " (2:12, 13).

But the full meaning of Joel's text is not exhausted in the near fulfillment of impending national disaster at the hand of the Babylonians. As we have already indicated by comparison of themes of Joel with similar passages of Ezekiel, Zephaniah, Matthew, and Revelation, the ultimate fulfillment of the intent of this text is in the final battle. The kingdom of King Jesus will come against the attempts of the wicked world leaders who wish to oppose his presence and against whose blandishments of unity the One who sits in heaven laughs in scornful derision (Ps. 2:14).

Even in that context of the impending end of the world there come the words of the Creator through his prophet Joel, " 'Even now, return . . . rend . . . return.' "

To the individual who has come to the end of a long, rebellious life, a life misspent and better not having been lived, there come the words of God in his indescribable mercy, " 'Even now, return . . . rend . . . return.' " To each person, as the thief on the cross or a G.I. in a foxhole under fire, there is still time to make peace with God. Joel recounts his words, "return . . . rend . . . return."

The Hebrew verb translated "return" is tantamount to the New Testament word "repent." It means to come back to God in the sense of coming back to reality, of accepting God's assessment of the nature of sin, of coming to grips with what it means to be a rebel against his mercy, of receiving his grace. To return to God properly must be a matter of the whole person; hence, Joel reports God's words, "with all your heart."

The accompanying actions of fasting, weeping, and mourning are the outward expressions of the inner reality. Fasting in biblical times was perceived as a voluntary, temporary withdrawal from the ordinary, expected, and divinely blessed pleasure of this world, as a means of quickening one's perception of divine reality. The pangs of hunger in fasting are prods to the person's mind to pray to God. Weeping and mourning are complementary terms speaking of the grief one feels when that person has truly come to face the enormity of his or her guilt, deserved because of the awfulness of sin.

The New Testament term "repent" bears much of the same ideas as the phrasing of this verse in Joel. To repent of sin is not a simple, light-hearted matter. Truly to repent is to feel deep remorse, to sense the reality of sin, to desire with all one's heart to move from that evil to righteousness.

Rend

Not only was Israel to return to God, the people of Jerusalem were also to rend their hearts, not just their garments (2:13). Again, the issue is one of inner reality, not just outward, physical expression. In Middle Eastern culture it was customary to tear at one's garments when expressing deep grief, such as at a time of bereavement. Even today, traditional Jewish and Arab people will tear a jacket pocket when hearing of the death of a loved one. In the West we are often conditioned to hold our feelings within, not to express them before others so openly. Yet a healthy aspect of some cultures is the outward, physical, tangible expression of these deep feelings.

An outward action is appropriate as a cultural expression of deep feeling. But, as with all outward actions, there is always the danger of tearing at the garment but never really feeling something within. Biblical piety always springs from within and has outward expressions of that inner reality.

Some have thought it was only in the teaching of Jesus that the inner reality of biblical faith was really expressed. In fact, as Joel demonstrates, the inner reality was always important to God. Joel says this, as do all the prophets. Jesus just emphasized it more fully, more beautifully.

Yahweh Your God

We are struck in this passage of Joel with the opportunity that God gives his sinning people to return to him, to rend their hearts. We are struck more profoundly though by the description of the God to whom they are to return. Here again are the words of verse 13,

> Return to Yahweh your God,
> for he is gracious and compassionate,

slow to anger and abounding in love,
and he relents from sending calamity.

First, we are reminded of the special significance of the name of God, Yahweh. The standard English versions render the Hebrew word as "LORD," with all four letters capitalized. "Lord," with capital "L" is the way English versions render the Hebrew word 'adōnāy (see Amos 3:13), which does mean "lord" in the sense of the one in charge, the master. But the conventional English use of the word "LORD" obscures for many readers that the underlying Hebrew word is a personal name for God. Yahweh, sometimes mistakenly given as "Jehovah," is the name by which God relates himself to his people. He is the eternal one who is dynamically present with his people, living for them and working for their good. It is a name of intense, profound, dynamic relationship. Here is the name of the God who has entered into personal covenant with his people.

The meaning of the name "Yahweh" is enhanced in Joel 2:13 by the words "your God." By this phrase the people of Israel are taken back to Mount Sinai, back to the thunder and the mercy, back to covenant, back to God. For the Hebrew person, the name "Yahweh your God" has the emotional and spiritual significance as the name "the Lord Jesus Christ" does for the Christian.

Gracious and Compassionate

Second, we are deeply impressed by these words of grace. Here we come to the heart of God. The expected definition of God in both Testaments is not his wrath, but his mercy. Wrath is God's strange, alien work (see Isa. 28:21). The judgmental wrath of God proceeds from his essential holiness, his abhorrence of sin, his righteous character. But his person is described in the words of Joel 2:13, "gracious and compassionate."

These two words are quite close in meaning, so that translators may give the same meaning for each of these words from time to time. The words together form what we term an hendiadys. This term comes from the Greek, meaning "one-through-two." That is, two similar words joined by a simple connective are used to enhance each other to give a potent meaning. The Hebrew words "gracious and compassionate" are regularly paired together, and their order may have either before the other (see Ps. 103:8, "compassionate and gracious," and Ps. 111:4, "gracious and compassionate").

The Hebrew word *hannûn*, "gracious," is one of those select few Hebrew words used only as an attribute of God in the Hebrew Bible. A specific example of the meaning of this word is found in Exodus 22:27 where the Almighty One, Creator of the universe, pledges he will hear the cry for help of an endebted man whose only possession, a cloak, is taken from him by his moneylender. "'When he cries out to me, I will hear, for I am compassionate (Hebrew, *hannûn*).'"

The second term is *rahûm*, a term related to the word for the womb, speaking of a deep, womblike compassion. This term suggests a comparison with a woman's love for her child, the most intense and lasting love we usually experience. The picture of the maternal love of Father God is a wondrous way of enhancing our appreciation of his love for his people.

When *rahûm*, "compassion," is adjoined to *hannûn*, "graciousness," the resultant meaning is something like "abundant compassion" or "deep graciousness." The words work together to enhance each other and to bring us near to the heart of God.

Anger and Love

Joel's description of the person of Yahweh does not deny his wrath nor sentimentalize his love. Rather, he presents the love and anger of God in the balance we learn to expect in the biblical text. His anger is short; his love abounds.

The Hebrew term translated "love" in this verse is one of the most expressive of Hebrew words to describe the character of God. This is the word *hesed*, a term that combines the ideas of mercy and love with the concept of loyalty. Some prefer to translate this word as "loving loyalty," or "loyal love," in an attempt to bring together these two excellencies that the word describes. The word *hesed* is a word of covenant, as is God's name Yahweh. These two terms ought to be known by Christian people. We have long learned to cherish the Greek word *agápe*, expressive of the self-giving love of God. Now it is time to add to our biblical vocabulary the luxuriant word of his loyal love, *ḥesed*.

He Relents

The climax of verse 13 is that it is possible that God may relent, may change his mind, about the approaching calamity. Perhaps, this is the most startling of all. We believe in the love and mercy of God. We are aware of his judgmental wrath, his strange work. But we assume that the wrath is inevitable because of the sin that is so very pernicious. Joel suggests that if the repentance of God's people were sincere, if their contrition were from within and not just from without, if there were truly a change of heart then God might relent from his pronouncement of calamity.

This is not a novel discovery for Joel. It is a subtheme in the prophets generally. In fact, this is a part of the story of the Book of Jonah. The reason that "flighty dove" of a prophet took off for worlds unknown in the opposite direction of Nineveh is that he knew what Yahweh was really like. He knew that if he were to preach the message of God's impending doom on Nineveh and if the people were to respond to the message in genuine repentance, Yahweh would relent and spare the people from the punishment that Jonah felt they deserved. This is Jonah's very complaint against God—he knew him too well!

> That is why I was so quick to flee to Tarshish. I knew that you are a gracious and compassionate God, slow to anger and abounding in love, a God who relents from sending calamity (Jonah 4:2).

Jonah's knowledge of God's grace discouraged him so much he desired to die because the nation he hated was spared. This knowledge was the same as that of Joel and the other prophets of Hebrew Scripture.

In all of this, we may be tempted to believe that Jonah and Joel have discovered something new about God, something unknown to the stern Moses, whom we associate with God's restrictions and regulations. In such a viewpoint we err, of course. For the words of Joel 2:13 and Jonah 4:2 are traced ultimately to Moses on Mount Sinai, clutching the second set of the tablets of the Law and seeing the glory of Yahweh coming near in the cloud. These are the words of Exodus 34:5–7,

> Then Yahweh came down in the cloud and stood there with him and proclaimed his name, Yahweh. And he passed in front of Moses, proclaiming, "Yahweh, Yahweh, *the compassionate and gracious God,* slow to anger, abounding in love and faithfulness, maintaining love to thousands, and forgiving wickedness, rebellion and sin. Yet he does not leave the guilty unpunished; he punishes the children and their children for the sin of the fathers to the third and fourth generation."

Based on the original revelation of Yahweh to Moses and buttressed by their own revelation of his character, the prophets of God were able to extend to people the promise of God's grace, even when it seemed that they were in the final extremity of their existence. There is always the possibility of Yahweh relenting if the people would only turn to him anew.

Who Knows?

Joel's recital of the grace of God in the midst of extreme displeasure ends in the remarkable rhetorical device, "Who knows? He may turn and have pity" (2:14a). There is a play on words in this colon. The verb translated "he may turn" is the same basic word as "return" used in verses 12 and 13. The people are to "return" to Yahweh; he will "turn" back to them. Here is a classic presentation of what the New Testament writers term "reconciliation." God and man, at odds because of the rebellions of sinful people, may now turn to each other and be friends again.

Readers of the New Testament are told that which the Old Testament believer only knew in small part. Only later do we learn that the basis on which God is able to turn from wrath to mercy is based on the completed work of the Lord Jesus Christ. In his death the wrath of God was fully expended and by his present life God reaches out to former enemies, no longer angry (see 2 Cor. 5:17–19).

I love the anticipation of this concept expressed in one of the hymns of Isaiah.

> In that day you will say:
> "I will praise you, O Yahweh,

> Although you were angry with me,
> your anger has turned away
> and you have comforted me" (Isa. 12:1).

And if God shall turn from anger to display his mercy again, then Joel says he will leave blessings instead of cursings. The materials for the grain and drink offerings will be restored (2:14). These last words from verse 14 tie in beautifully with the themes of Joel 1:13. Because of the plague of locusts, there were no longer the offerings of grain and wine to present before Yahweh in holy worship. In the calamity that Joel 2 describes, there will be a cutting off of all agriculture as well. But if the people were to turn back to God, and he to them, the agricultural devastation would be replaced by plenty. Blessing would cover cursing; peace triumph over war.

A Time for Prayer

Earlier in this chapter we noted that Joel 2:12–17 has two subsections to it. The first, Joel 2:12–14, centers on the person and the character of God, who still offers mercy and deliverance to his sinning people. The second, Joel 2:15–17, presents to the people under certain judgment a plan of action that may help them to avert his wrath, "even now."

The second subsection, Joel 2:15–17, begins with a literary tie to two earlier portions of the book: the call for trumpets and the call for a sacred assembly. In Joel 2:15, the Lord's instruction is to have the trumpets blown to initiate a sacred fast; whereas in Joel 2:1 the trumpets were to be blown to warn the people of impending judgment. The first call for a sacred fast was to the priests who had experienced the invasion of locusts (1:13); the second call for a sacred fast is to the people who live on the precipice of the final war, the last battle, the Day of Yahweh.

The call of God is for the entire nation, from elders to babes still nursing at their mothers' breasts. Moreover, the call of God is without exception. Even a bride and bridegroom should leave their chambers of anticipated marital bliss and forego their honeymoon until the prayers of God's people are answered. For what purpose would a bridal night be if the Day of Yahweh were to descend before the couple even neared each other?

Spare Your People

Joel even instructs the priests how to pray in verse 17. But then we remember that he was a man well-experienced in prayer himself (see 1:19–20). The priests were to pray from the temple, weeping as they prayed and beseeching the Lord to spare his people, to protect his land, and to maintain his reputation among the nations as one who defends his own people against all assault.

In the words of verse 17 we learn several things about the prayer that Joel believed would be effective with God. First, there is propriety because the effective prayers would be from the priests centered in the temple and based upon true remorse. Second, the prayer was to be based both on the mercy of God and his reputation. Yahweh's mercy is between himself and his people; his reputation concerns the way others who are outside learn to think of him. Joel urges prayer from both motivations.

For if God were to spare his people, it would be an act of consummate mercy and a work of maintaining the record of his faithfulness to his people before a watching world.

It is with these wistful words in hope of grace that the first division of the Book of Joel ends. Joel 1:1–2:17 is the first major part of our book, a presentation of the plague of locusts which gives a foreboding warning of the approaching Day of Yahweh. In Joel 2:18 the second half of the book begins, and with that verse, so will our next lesson.

For Further Study

1. How does the content of Joel 2:12-17 heighten the beauty of these words? Can you find another text or two that have similarly abrupt changes of wrath and mercy in the prophets?

2. How does Joel maintain the balance between the wrath and the mercy of God?

3. Joel's instruction, in the face of God's impending wrath, is for the priests to lead the nation in a sacred fast, a time of prayer and weeping before the Lord (Joel 2:15-17). What implication may there be for our own national destiny in the face of overwhelming sin?

Chapter 7

In a Future Tense
(Joel 2:18–27)

Perspective

Joel 2:18 begins the second major section of this potent little book. The first section, 1:2–2:17, was animated by the excruciating events the nation of Judah experienced in an unparalleled invasion of locusts during the time of the prophet Joel of Jerusalem (1:2–12). This locust invasion became the prompting for the prophet to speak of a future time of devastation that would make the present calamity recede into a dim memory of comparative unpleasantness (2:1–11). Yet in both the experience of Judah's present distress (1:13–20) and in the future day of overwhelming disaster (2:12–17), there remain God's pleas. He asks his people to return to him, to rend their hearts, and to restore fellowship with him because in all his grace he is ever willing to work in mercy to the good of them.

With Joel 2:18 we are cast into the future tense as we read about God's determination to bring about the realization of his promises of blessing and wonder. But in this future tense there are numerous contacts with the present. This is the way of the prophets, to relate the future to the present so that people of all ages will sense the relevance of their words. The material of this section grows out of both the distress of the present time, the locust invasion, and the distress of the future time, the final battle. There will come final glory in the pattern of God's prophetic word: first the worst, then the best.

The first portion of this section presents an anticipative of

71

God's answer to his people's pleas (2:18–20); the second issues a future call for praise to God who will have delivered his people and his land (2:21–24), and the third speaks of the reasons for God's restoration of his land and his people (2:25–27). We begin with the anticipation that is rooted in the jealousy of God. In fact, we will linger on the idea of jealousy because of its prime importance in our text.

Divine Jealousy

Usually when we think of the word "jealousy," we think of the destructive attitudes and vindictive actions of a jilted lover, actions and attitudes that may lead to physical abuse and moral outrageousness. Put simply, the term "jealousy" is not often regarded as a positive word in our experience.

At the same time, we know what it means to be jealous. All of us, I suspect, from time to time have feelings of jealousy. It may begin early when brothers and sisters count the little things in their Christmas stockings and check out any parental miscalculations on fairness. It might be when the first love of childhood is dashed against the fickle nature of children as a girl friend or boyfriend dumped us for the guy (gal) in the cool blue sweater. Sometimes feelings of jealousy come from resentments over the betterment of our neighbors, the promotion of a co-worker, or a new car spotted down the block. We often have the feeling that the other is undeserving, that we should have the better home, the better job, the nicer car.

Christians are not exempt from these feelings. They are common feelings from urges bubbling deep within our humanity. I have heard some preachers say that the way to avoid the covetousness of jealousy is to say something like, "I wish you had something even better yet, as I wish I had what you have." Yet this seems to be only a removal of a degree of the basic problem of jealousy. Even pastors cast a longing eye to another pastor's seemingly easier charge or more pleasant section of God's vineyard. More than one pastor has coveted his brother's larger office, and not a few his brother's prettier wife. This evil affects us all. Jealousy and envy are the most pernicious afflictions of our fallen humanity.

At root, jealousy of this type is a breaking of the tenth

commandment. It is a desiring for oneself what belongs to another. The promptings for jealousy are avarice and greed. Jealousy is an expression of the worst in a person, not the best.

How then, we may ask, do we read that Yahweh, God of reality, experiences jealousy? Here are the words of our text.

> Then Yahweh will be jealous for his land
> and take pity on his people (2:18).

Zeal and Pity

A basic part of the interpretive task is not to prejudge the meaning of words. All of the feelings and emotions we use to describe the word "jealousy" may be far afield from the intention of the biblical writer who uses this word with God as the subject. Hence, we cannot bring our understanding of words to the text; we need to read out the understanding of a word from the writer's point of view.

One way to find the author's meaning of a word is to search the environment of that word for cues to its meaning. That is, the meaning of a given word is in the environment, the context, of its usage. Since we are reading Hebrew poetry in the Book of Joel, we may find the parallel wording of Hebrew style to be a tremendous aid for our understanding.

The first colon of Joel 2:18 uses the term "will be [became] jealous"; the second, "take [and] pity." Whatever is meant by the words of the first colon should have some essential bearing on the words of the second. Indeed, one of the ways of biblical poetry is to say in the first colon, "this is so," and then to add in the balancing words of the second colon, "what's more, so is this!" That is, there is a movement from the one to the second that is coherent, direct, and significant. The meaning of the first colon is regularly enhanced by the words of the second. Hence, the words "take pity" will help us to understand the words "will be jealous."

The Hebrew word translated "take pity" is from the root *ḥāmal*. One basic meaning for this verb is "to spare." A literal use of this verb is given in Jeremiah 50:14 in a prophetic taunt against the great enemy Babylon when she will finally be under assault from her own enemies. The prophet says to the attackers of that evil city, " 'Shoot at her! *Spare* no arrows, / for she has sinned against Yahweh.' "

The second basic meaning for this verb is "to have compassion," "to feel pity." It is this second meaning that our text demands. This verb is used, for example, in the story when baby Moses was found by Pharoah's daughter. The Hebrew male child, under the threat of death, had been left in a basket among the reeds along the bank of the River Nile, with the hope of his parents that he would not be discovered during the day. But the daughter of Pharaoh along with numerous attendants came to that very place on the Nile. There she intended to bathe. When she saw the basket, she sent a maiden to fetch it. When she lifted the cover off the basket, she saw the baby. The Bible says, "He was crying, and she felt sorry for him." The very verb translated "felt sorry" is the same verb as in Joel 2:18, "to take pity."

The deep, mysterious, maternal instincts of Pharoah's young daughter overcame her revulsion of a hated people and her knowledge of her father's determination that they suffer genocide. All she saw in that little basket was a weeping child, a helpless baby. And she felt something so profound that she was compelled to reach out, to touch, to caress, to embrace, to care for, and to protect. It was her feeling of compassion, of native pity, that caused Pharoah's daughter to disobey the law of her father's land, not only to spare the life of the little child, but also to adopt the child as her own. This deep sense of innate compassion is the meaning of the Hebrew word *hāmal*.

The word associated with this term for compassion in Joel 2:18 is *qāna'*, a verb that may be used for personal, vindictive anger based upon a sense of envy and covetousness. One very human example of this verb used in this way occurs in the story of the patriarch Jacob and his two wives Leah and Rachel. At one point the barren Rachel was so jealous (the verb is *qāna'*) of the children born to her sister Leah that she screamed out to their husband Jacob, " 'Give me children, or I'll die!' " (Gen. 30:1).

But this word *qāna'* can also mean a zeal for the right thing that brings one to selfless actions of great daring. I think, for example, of the story of Phinehas son of Eleazar in the aftermath of the Balaam story (Num. 22–24). This young man was so consumed with zeal for the honor of Yahweh that he rammed his spear through the copulating bodies of an idolatrous couple whose actions were not only prolonging the plague on the people but condemning the glory of God. His actions turned away the wrath of God in the amazing word play of Numbers 25:10. There we hear the words of Yahweh approving the zeal of this young man with respect to the zeal of Yahweh:

> "Phinehas son of Eleazar, the son of Aaron, the priest, has turned my anger away from the Israelites; for he was as zealous as I am for my honor among them, so that in my zeal I did not put an end to them."

God's Feelings

In Joel 2:18 we sense the zeal of Yahweh to do the right thing for his land, just as we sense the compassion of Yahweh to do the right thing for his people. Here these words qāna', "to be jealous," and hāmal, "to feel compassion," are splendidly paired together. In these words we *feel* the emotions of God in ways that are understandable to us because they are so much like our own.

It may seem strange to speak of "the emotions of God." Theologians speak of this type of language as *anthropopathism*, attributing to God the emotions of man. Yet we do not wish by such a label to conclude that the emotions are not genuine, that this is just an attribution we make of God rather than something really a part of him. Since God has revealed himself to man as a Person, we should expect that the description of personality include feelings. If the terms for those feelings are human terms, that is just so we may understand them and relate to them. The feelings of God are the sublime expression of his Person. They are surely beyond our own experience or understanding. But they are real.

The "zeal" or "jealousy" of Yahweh (qāna' may be translated either way) is especially indicated with reference to the feelings of the Lord with respect to the land of Judah and the city of Jerusalem. Zechariah the prophet reports an angelic announcement of the word of Yahweh, "I am very zealous (qāna') for Jerusalem and Zion (Zech. 1:14)." Again in Zechariah we find the verb *qāna'* in the words of Yahweh, "I am very jealous for Zion; I am burning with jealousy for her" (Zech. 8:2).

All of this goes back to Torah, to the instruction of Moses concerning the meaning of the land in the perception of Yahweh. Deuteronomy 11:12 reads,

> It is a land Yahweh your God cares for; the eyes of Yahweh your God are continually on it from the beginning of the year to its end.

No wonder we have learned to call the land of Canaan, the place of Israel, the "holy land." It is holy, separated, and made particular to God himself. Of no other land may these words be said. Hence, the jealousy of Yahweh for his land is to be explained in his special pleasure that he finds there.

While the judgment that comes upon the people who live in Jerusalem is provoked by their disregard for the ways and works of God, nonetheless, God's jealousy for that land and place compels him to seek it out again, to preserve and restore Zion as the place of his dwelling, the expression of his glory.

New Grain, New Wine

Yahweh thus promises that he will respond to the prayers of the people in their dejection and distress. He will once again make the land of his choice experience the productivity of his promise. He will bring again the grain, wine, and oil, which the people lost in the invasion of locusts (1:2–12), and which the people were to lose again during the time of the invasion of the devastating army (2:1–11).

There is a lovely coming round of the circle in the words of Joel 2:19. All that was lost will be restored. Grain, wine, and oil will once again be enjoyed fully, and never again will the Lord bring upon his people the distress of time past. His zeal for the land and his pity for the people assure that trouble is not the last word for them, only a passing word. Blessing is coming because of the deep feelings God has for his people, his land, and the commitment he has to his own promises. In these words we are drawn close to the heart of God.

The Northern Army

Because of the particulars of the geography of the land of Israel, most invaders would come from the North. There was always the threat of assault from the South, of course. Egypt remained a threat throughout all of Israel's existence. But time after time the invasions of Canaan came from the North. This was true even if the homeland of the invaders were way off to the East. The great desert regions east of Canaan made it nearly impossible for an army to march and be supplied by a direct assault westward on Canaan. These armies would all circle up what Breasted long ago called the "fertile crescent," and follow the waterways of Mesopotamia and the great highways connecting the cities of those regions. Then they would fall southward on Samaria and Judah as a stone plummeting down a crevasse.

Joel 2:20 describes God's promise of destruction of the "northern army." This may be a promise to destroy the army of Babylon, which carried out the destruction of Jerusalem in 587/586 B.C. It may also refer to the end-time assault on the land of Israel from the North by the armies mysteriously termed Gog, Meshech, and Tubal (see Ezek. 38–39). This verse may also be a general promise of God's ultimate victory over all Israel's foes, with the expression "the northern army" a suitable generalization because of the normal route of conquest.

God's intention is to drive all invaders of his land into the desert, which they so steadfastly avoid, with columns routed into the eastern sea (the Dead Sea) and the western sea (the Mediterranean), and the stench of the corpses an assault to the senses. Such a verse, so unpalatable to modern sensitivities, was a joy to those who read it, for it told them that ultimately there will be an end of evil, and end of oppression, and end of destruction of the land and the people of God. We should greet the promise of God to end all oppression and evil with the same relief this word brought in olden days. At last, the land will be ridded of foes. Their foul stench turns sweet when we think that no more will they trouble God's land.

Great Things

The last colon of verse 20 is somewhat troublesome. The NIV translates these words, "Surely he has done great things."

But because of the incongruity of attributing to the evil northern army these positive words, the NIV has printed them as though they belong with the following verse, with God as their subject. These scholars may have taken their hint from the last colon of verse 21, "Surely Yahweh has done great things." You will see this as you look at your copy of the NIV.

I believe the NKJV has resolved this issue in a more satisfactory manner. The last colon of verse 20, attributing great things to the northern army, seems to have no textual uncertainty in the original Hebrew. It is best taken as a genuine part of this verse, not the beginning of verse 21. Yet it is certainly contrastive in meaning with the last colon of verse 21, which attributes "great things" to Yahweh. Hence, there is likely a play on words in these two verses. The NKJV translates the phrase in verse 20 to relate to the northern army, "Because he has done monstrous things," and the last words in verse 21 to relate to God, "For Yahweh has done marvelous things." The Hebrew ear and eye love these turns of phrases. In this case the very same words are used for diametrically opposed ideas: monstrous things and marvelous things, the monstrous things of the enemy and the marvelous things of the Lord.

Fear Not

Usually when we read, "Do not be afraid" in the Bible, we think about people who are being comforted by the Lord. But in Joel 2:21 and again in 2:22, it is the elements of the land and nature that are told no longer to fear. These are touching expressions, where the land itself is told to transform its fear into joy, and animals are to cease to fear because of the coming of the productive green of the pastures again.

The imagery of these verses takes us back to the locust invasions in chapter 1 and the groaning of the land we described in our discussion of Joel 1:10, "the land mourns." No longer must the land mourn or the earth fear. For joy has come. Such language is not unusual in the poetic portions of the Bible. Psalm 97, for example, calls for the earth to be glad and the distant shores to rejoice (Ps. 97:1) because of the coming reign of the Lord.

Of course, whenever the heavens or the earth, whenever

animals or vegetation are told to rejoice, the ultimate intent is for God's people to take joy. The first couplet of verse 23 of Joel 2 brings this home.

> Be glad, O people of Zion,
> rejoice in Yahweh your God.

The same words used to compel the land to be glad and rejoice (v. 21) are now used for the people (v. 23). These two synonyms, "be glad and rejoice," are another example of *hendiadys,* as we have seen in earlier portions of our study. These two words, close synonyms joined by the simple connective, present one concept: "rejoice exceedingly."

Rains and the Teacher

The reason for the rejoicing of the people of Zion in the day of Yahweh's pleasure is the return of bounty to the land. This renewal of agriculture, so important in the context of the devastation of chapter 1, is in the future tense. It speaks of the coming time of plenty when the parched land becomes the garden of the Lord's bounty. Many Christians believe this time to be the future kingdom of the Savior Jesus Christ, the time of the Lord's smile upon the land and his people.

Joel 2:23 has a very difficult line to translate. This is the second couplet of the verse where early printings of the NIV read that God has given "a teacher for righteousness." Readers who are familiar with the so-called Dead Sea Scrolls, or the texts from Qumran, will readily recall this phrase. The founder and principal teacher of that sect of Jewish people was called the Teacher of Righteousness, a messianic title applied to their great guru. That phrase comes from this text, Joel 2:23.

The Hebrew words are not clear, however. Early printings of the NIV margin read, "Or / *in righteousness the autumn rains.*" In more recent printings of the NIV the situation is reversed. The text has the words of autumn rains and in the margin the words of the teacher for righteousness. The NKJV does the same. In the text the NKJV reads, "the former rain faithfully," but in its margin reads, "or *teacher of righteousness.*"

The issue here is not one of a disputed reading of the

Hebrew text; it is a dispute concerning how the Hebrew text is
to be translated. The Hebrew word in question is not the word
translated "righteousness" (or, "faithfully" as in NKJV), but the
accompanying word *ha-môreh*. This term may mean "the
teacher" or "the autumn/former rains." That is, there are two
separate entries in the Hebrew dictionaries, each with the same
spelling, but each with quite different meanings.

The word *môreh* certainly means "early rain/autumn rain"
in Psalm 84:6, where the phrasing "the autumn rains also cover
it with pools" is used in a parallel construction to the phrase "a
place of springs." More importantly, the word *môreh* certainly
means "autumn rains" at the end of Joel 2:23, where it is paired
with the term for spring rains (Hebrew, *malqôsh*). That the word
has the meaning "autumn rains" within this same verse is
certainly significant.

On the other hand, the word *môreh* means "teacher" in the
place name of Genesis 12:6, "the great tree of Moreh" or "the
Oak of the Teacher," the site near Shechem where Abraham
made his camp and altar to Yahweh. In Job 36:22, *môreh* is used
in the phrase, "Who is a teacher like him [God]?" You may wish
to see also Proverbs 5:13 and Isaiah 30:20 for other examples of
this word meaning "teacher."

Our decision as to the meaning of the word *môreh* in Joel
2:23 may come from our sense of the most likely association
with the phrases in the environment of the verse. That is, were
there another phrase in this verse that presented a balancing
line, such as "a speaker of truth" or "a ruler in faithfulness,"
then we would feel very comfortable with the meaning "a
teacher for/of righteousness." In fact, we would love such an
expression, for it seems especially apt as a description of the
Messiah, of the Lord Jesus.

But if the words in the surrounding context speak of rain
and showers, then the meaning for the disputed word seems
more likely to be another term of rain. Indeed, the rest of this
verse, and of the entire flow of meaning from verse 21–24,
speaks of the renewal of rain and the attendant blessings that
will come from God in the showers from his hand.

The point of this section surely is that God has renewed his
covenantal blessings with the land. Deuteronomy 11:13–15 is

one of several texts that explains the association of the autumn and the spring rains as the blessing of Yahweh on the land in response to the faithfulness of the people in obedience to his commands. A day is coming, Joel describes, when the rains will return in the fullness of God's blessing. This line of reasoning seems pretty convincing that the word *môreh* in the second colon of our verse be translated as "autumn rains."

Yet, here is another approach that may give some reason to stay with the original reading of the NIV text. The Hebrew writers love using plays on words, as we have repeatedly discovered. The context of this section is one of the return of rains and the renewal of covenant. The basic word for the covenant in the Old Testament is *tôrah*, "teaching." The teaching demands a teacher; *tôrah* proceeds from *ha-môreh*. Hence, the unexpected wording in this verse, "for he has given you a teacher for righteousness," may be precisely the point of this passage.

What a pleasant surprise it would be to find in verses dealing with rain this subtle, but significant, title for our Savior. For surely it is he who is the Teacher for righteousness.

Two grammatical issues present themselves to lend some support to this viewpoint. First, the term we have discussed appears without the article when it means "autumn rains" at the end of the verse; it is used with the article in the phrase under discussion. Second, the phrase "the autumn rains *for/of right-eousness*" does not so easily convert to the marginal reading of the NIV, *"in righteousness* the autumn rains" or the text of the NKJV, *"the former rain faithfully."* The full phrase *ha-môreh liṣāqâ* reads quite easily, "the teacher of/for righteousness."

Hence, the prophet Joel may have given us an exquisite, delicate, surprising expression, based on a word play that is delightful. In sum, what I have done is to adjust to the more recent printings of the NIV. The contextual evidence works strongly for "autumn rains." That Jewish interpreters at Qumran understood "teacher of righteousness" suggests this is also a viable, but less likely, rendering. In a context of the return of rain and the renewal of covenant, there is the presentation of the giving of the teacher of righteousness. Christian readers know who that person surely must be, the Lord Jesus Christ. Because of the dispute concerning the translation of this phrase, this is not a strong verse to use in argumentation. But because of the subtle beauty of the text, it most certainly calls for reverent reflection and deep devotion.

Divine Recompense

Yahweh's words in Joel 2:25 are marvelously suitable for the future tense perspective of this section of the book. The experience of the people of Joel's day in the locust invasion was their preoccupation. But Yahweh promises that one day there will be his repayment. God will make all things right, as they ought to be. The words used by Joel in 1:4 to describe the terrors of the four successive invasions of locusts are used anew in this verse to give a sense of having come full circle. The words for these various locusts are exactly the same as in the earlier text, but in a slightly different order. In an earlier section we noted the difficulties in the translation of these words. Here we may simply list the various Hebrew words for different orders of locusts to display their order in these two passages.

Joel 1:4 has this order:	Joel 2:25 has this order:
ha-gāzām	ha-'arbeh
ha-'arbeh	ha-yeleq
ha-yeleq	he-ḥāsîl
he-ḥāsîl	ha-gāzām

It is only in the end of the verse that we read the disturbing, yet perhaps expected words, "'my great army which I sent to you.'" It is only at the end of the story that we learn the divine perspective.

Praise and Plenty

It is the intention of the Lord to use the restoration of the land, and the gracious provisions to his people, for two basic ends: their plenty and his praise. The words of verse 26 relating to the enjoyment of plenty of food, leading to the praise of God, is a reiteration of the covenantal promise and provision explained in Deuteronomy 6:10-12. When the people have enjoyed the plenty of the land, then they were to remember

Yahweh, honor him and serve him, for it is he who is the giver of the gifts of plenty.

So the people who will enjoy the plenty in the days to come are to join in the praise of his name, for it will be he who has worked wonders and who will spare his people from further shame.

All this works toward the finale of our section as God says to his people,

> "Then you will know that I am in Israel,
>   that I am Yahweh your God,
>   and that there is no other;
>   never again will my people be shamed" (2:27).

We will see more of what it means to live in the presence of God in our next chapter, the study of Joel 2:28-32. For the present, it is sufficient to be impressed with the spirited movement from the jealousy and pity of Yahweh at the beginning of this section to the abiding presence of Yahweh described at the end. Here is stirring theology. The Book of Joel may begin with troubles caused by disagreeable insects. But this little, grand book takes us into the presence of the Creator whose dwelling will one day be with his people in his land.

For Further Study

1. Read again Joel 2:15-19. Observe both connections and disconnections. Do you see why verse 17 ends one section and verse 18 starts the next? Yet do you see ways in which these verses flow from one to the other?

2. The jealousy of God is articulated in the Ten Commandments. Turn to Exodus 20 (and Deuteronomy 5) to determine the nature of that jealousy. Then relate this concept to the central words of God's relationship with his people in Deuteronomy 6:1-15.

3. Reflect on the phrase, *the emotions of God.* Use a Bible concordance and a Bible dictionary to develop a list of passages on this topic and the emotions they present.

4. Use a good Bible atlas (*The Moody Bible Atlas*, or *The Macmillan Bible Atlas* are good choices) to locate the general roads of travel in Palestine in ancient times. Find why the

geography demanded that most armies who marched against
Jerusalem would come from the north.

5. Can you think of or find other passages in Scripture
where there is a recapitulation of a verse similar to the interplay
of Joel 2:25 and 1:4?

Chapter 8

The Outpouring of the Spirit
(Joel 2:28-32)

Pentecost

Fifty days after Passover comes the Jewish festival of Pentecost. Fifty days after the Passover festival during which the Lord Jesus was put to death, then rose from the grave, came the festival of Pentecost when the Church of Jesus Christ was born. Acts 2, which describes that day, is one of the most dramatic passages in the Bible.

On that day, over the city of Jerusalem and upon the gathered people who were believers in the ascended Christ, there came the sound of a sudden swoosh of a violent wind blowing, it seemed, from very heaven. The sound rushed into the room where they were sitting. Then fire appeared, and it began dividing. It was as though this fire took the shape of tongues, and these fire-tongues came to rest on each of them. Then they were all filled with the Holy Spirit, in proof of which marvel, these people began to speak in languages they had never learned.

When the apostle Peter preached his great sermon in Jerusalem that Sunday morning, he had an explanation for the bizarre and marvelous behavior of his friends. The sound of their speaking was not the staggering sounds of drunks, as some supposed. These people had not been drinking so very early on that morning!

The languages that were heard by the cosmopolitan visitors to the crowded city of Jerusalem that morning were being

spoken by a variety of persons who had been specially enabled
by the filling of the Holy Spirit. For biblical proof of his
explanation of these stunning phenomena, Peter quoted from
the words of Joel 2:28-32 (see Acts 2:17-21).

We have good reason to believe, therefore, that Joel 2:28-32
is of signal importance for an understanding of God's new work
among his people the church, of the biblical teaching on the
person and work of the Holy Spirit, and of the nature of end
times. It is also an exceedingly important text in the flow of the
Book of Joel.

The Setting

Joel 2:28-32 is a tightly written, self-contained unit within
the Book of Joel. In fact, in the Hebrew Bible these verses form
a separate chapter. The last verse in chapter 2 in the Hebrew
Bible is verse 27. The verses of 2:28-32 in the English Bible
appear as chapter 3 verses 1-5 in Hebrew. The third chapter in
the English text is chapter 4 in Hebrew. There are the very same
number of verses, and the same sequence in both texts, just a
different numbering pattern.

Joel 2:28 begins with the phrase, "And afterward," words
which Peter cites as, "In the last days." The context for these
words is found in the preceding section, Joel 2:18-27. We have
already seen that this particular text presents the fullness of the
coming of the divine kingdom on earth, the time when God will
dwell with man. We recall the closing words of that section.

> "Then you will know that I am in Israel,
>   that I am Yahweh your God,
>   and that there is no other;
> never again will my people be shamed" (2:27).

These are the words of promise of the coming of the King.
They are in the context of the healing of the land, the restoration
of the people, the blessing of God's forgiveness, and the promise
that never again will there be reason for the shaming of his
people. These are the days many Christians believe to be the
period of the millennial rule of the Lord Jesus Christ as noted in
Revelation 20:1-6, but described in numerous Old Testament
prophecies, such as this one in Joel.

The setting for the prophecy of the outpouring of the Holy Spirit in the Book of Joel, then, is the time of the presence of God in the midst of his people, the time of the coming of his kingdom and his presence to the earth. The Hebrew prophet Ezekiel also speaks of the coming of the outpouring of the Holy Spirit of God on the house of Israel (Ezek. 39:29). As in the case of Joel, Ezekiel presents this prophecy in the context of the future, glorious kingdom of the Savior on earth (see Ezek. 39:25-29). The time of the outpouring of the Spirit in these prophetic utterances is the time of the kingdom of God on earth.

The Mystery

One of the most important observations to make in this text is that the speaker is God himself. It is Yahweh who speaks beginning in Joel 2:19 (with introductory words in verse 18), and it is he who is speaking in verses 28-32. Peter also is aware that it is God who speaks in these verses of Joel, for he introduces his quotation of the words of Joel by saying, " 'God says' " (Acts 2:17).

What God does say is that he will pour out his Spirit on all people (Joel 2:28). When these words were first spoken through Joel of Jerusalem, they must have caused some considerable consternation among those who first pondered their meaning. The revelation of God in triunity—God as Father, Son, and Holy Spirit—is distinctly a New Testament development. There are Old Testament passages here and there, and Joel 2:28 is one of them, where there are hints that the God of Israel, who is One, is not simple but complex. As the old formula has it: one God, three persons.

Likely there is no more difficult a teaching in the Bible than that of the nature of the Holy Trinity. It is because our mortal, time-and-space-bound minds have trouble understanding God's revelation of himself in this manner that we like to call this a mystery. As a mystery, we may give assent to the reality of the person of one God in three persons, even though we do not really have adequate models of explanation. In the final analysis, we ask ourselves if a God would really be God who could be fully understandable to us.

Here in Joel 2:28, we hear the words of Yahweh (here taken

to be the Father) saying, " 'I will pour out my Spirit.' " This is uncanny. It is a mystery, a wonder of the reality of God.

We are reminded as well of the words of the Lord Jesus who said to his disciples that he would ask the Father, " 'and he will give you another Counselor to be with you forever—the Spirit of truth' " (John 14:16, 17). It is only as we piece these various strands of the teaching of Scripture together that we begin to realize that Yahweh of Israel is the Father, the Son and the Holy Spirit of Christian revelation.

Usually when we read "Yahweh" in the Old Testament, we are to think of God, undifferentiated in his person. At times when we read "Yahweh" in the Hebrew Bible, we are to think of God the Father. One example is Psalm 110:1, "Yahweh says to my Lord." The Lord Jesus interprets this verse as the Father speaking to him (see Matt. 22:41–45). There are also times that the word "Yahweh" speaks specifically of the Lord Jesus Christ. For example, the vision that Isaiah had of Yahweh seated high and on his heavenly throne is interpreted by John to be a revelation of the Lord Jesus (compare John 12:37–41).

In Joel 2:28, it is Yahweh (the Father) who promises to pour out his Spirit on all flesh. This promise of God figures in the teaching of the Lord Jesus who prays for this outpouring of the Spirit, anticipating the Father to send the Counselor, the Spirit of truth to his disciples (John 14:15–17).

The promise of the outpouring of the Holy Spirit in Joel 2:28–32 has two major thrusts. It is universal among God's people, and it is associated with the coming Day of Yahweh.

The Content

The first great teaching concerning the outpouring of the Holy Spirit is its universalism among the people of God. The promise of the pouring out of the Holy Spirit upon all people is made specific in the next phrases of Joel's prophetic words (2:28–29). The outpouring of the Spirit will result in the gifting of all manner of the people of God in prophetic utterances. The outflow of the Spirit is generous and gracious, and altogether unexpected.

There is a beautiful, stylistic aspect to this text because it begins and ends in similar wording. We call this sort of thing an *inclusio,* a frame that sets off the central words. Verse 28 begins, "And afterward, / I will pour out my Spirit on all people." Verse 29 ends, "I will pour out my Spirit in those days." By this very similiar beginning and ending, the central words are made even more prominent—and prominent they should be.

The promise of the coming of the Spirit to the people of God is without distinction of person. Ancient and modern barriers of sex, age, and class are broken. The democratization and the egalitarianism of biblical religion have deep roots in this glorious prophecy of God in the writing of Joel. The New Testament passages that speak of oneness in Christ, apart from issues of sex, class or national identity (see Gal. 3:28; Col. 3:11) have their spiritual roots in Joel 2.

The outpouring of the Spirit is apart from all barriers

- of gender: "'your sons and daughters'" (2:28), "'both men and women'" (2:29);
- of age: "'your old men ... your young men'" (2:28);
- of class: "'even on my servants'" (3:29).

The outpouring of the Spirit is inclusive of numerous wonders of prophetic utterance that

- they will prophesy (2:28);
- they will dream dreams (2:28);
- they will see visions (2:28).

These words of the inclusiveness of the wonders and of those who will experience them are truly remarkable, particularly in the period of time when they were uttered. The Old Testament world was largely marked by patriarchy, the rule of the father, and was consequently male-oriented. Israel was an exception to this general pattern from time to time, for she had women who were prophetesses, sages, and nobles, as well as great women who were wives and mothers in dignity of person and accomplishment in piety.

The general tendencies, however, even in Israel, were toward male-orientation of spiritual things. Joel 2:28–29 twice affirms that the outpouring of the Holy Spirit will be inclusive of women as well as men. The biblical doctrine of the spiritual gifts is informed by this reality. The gifts of the Spirit are for women as well as for men, for the aged as well as the young, the lower classes as well as the elite. This is a truly remarkable passage!

The Day of Yahweh

The second great revelation concerning the outpouring of the Holy Spirit is its association with the coming of the Day of Yahweh. We learn this truth in verses 30–31. It turns out that the outpouring of the Holy Spirit does not just affect the people of God. There are also ramifications of this outpouring that affect heaven and earth (2:30).

Among the signs of the coming of the Spirit are wonders on earth as well as omens in the heavenly bodies. These several phenomena include blood, fire, billows of smoke, as well as stunning reversals in the light factors of the sun and the moon. These expressions are a part of the vocabulary of eschatology, the biblical doctrine of the end times. They present the time of the end, which is the time of God's new beginning. These words remind us of several similiar expressions in the teaching of Jesus and the Book of Revelation about end times.

The clinching phrase comes at the end of verse 31,

> ". . . before the coming of the great
> and dreadful day of Yahweh."

These words take us back to Joel 1:15, 2:1–2, 11. The modifying words, "the great and dreadful," form another pair of words we term *hendiadys*." That is, it is not that the day is first "great" and then also "dreadful." What we have is one concept expressed through two terms, such as "greatly dreadful," or "dreadfully great."

The term "dreadful" is a passive participle related to the Hebrew verb root *yārē'*, "to fear," "to be awesome." This word is used at times to describe the person of God as a person of wonder and awe. Psalm 47:2, for example, reads,

> How *awesome* is Yahweh Most High,
> the great King over all the earth.

When this term is used for the Day of Yahweh, as in Joel 2:11 and 2:31, it is descriptive of horror and dread rather than wonder and awe. But the associations of the outpouring of the Holy Spirit in the latter passage help to transform and expand our understanding of the nature of this day.

When preparations were nearing completion for the final festivities of the Olympic Games in Los Angeles in 1984, one of the members of the planning committee was quoted as saying, "The final program will be so awesome it will rival the Second Coming." This man's misguided use of language transcends the expected excesses of publicity "hype." He cheapened the Olympics Finale by using arrogant blasphemy. One needs to sit before the prophets, such as Joel, to gain a perspective on language and truth concerning the time of the end.

The Day of Yahweh has its judgmental as well as its gracious aspects. It begins as a day of terror and judgment, as we have seen in our study of Joel 2:1–11. But it is also inclusive of the happily expected period following that judgment, initiating the time of the grace of God in the kingdom he establishes, as its use in Joel 2:30–31 indicates. That is the way of the expression, "the Day of Yahweh." Just when we think we are gaining a handle on the nature of that day, we discover a new aspect. Actually, the Day of Yahweh is also a day of great salvation.

Salvation

Joel's third great teaching concerning the time of the outpouring of the Holy Spirit is that it will be associated with a time of great salvation (Joel 2:32). The words "to call upon the name of Yahweh" in this verse have a particular significance in biblical thought. To call upon God is not just the raising of one's voice at a time of trouble to utter a random, "Oh-my-god," as one hears so commonly today in our culture. In fact, the Hebrew verb translated "to call" is more than to pray. The basic meaning of this verb is "to call out."

When qāra', "to call out," is used in association with the expression, "the name Yahweh," it involves what we may describe this side of the cross as "saving faith."

To call on the name Yahweh is to make proclamation in his name. It is to pray to him, but it is also to preach on his behalf. When Abram (later, "Abraham") built his first altars in Canaan, first at Shechem, and then near the area of Bethel and Ai, he

made proclamation in the name Yahweh (see Gen. 12:8). Here
he used the name Yahweh in true personal worship. He also
used the name Yahweh in bold evangelism, for he called out
that name in the presence of the Canaanites who then lived in
that land. He made himself known as the man who proclaims
the name Yahweh; that is, there was a personal identification
between himself and the God whose name he proclaimed.

When we read of making proclamation of the name Yahweh
in Joel 2:32, these several associations should be in our minds.
Here is an expression in the Hebrew Scriptures for one who
confesses the reality of God, and the need for the work of that
God in one's own life. Scripture says such will be saved. To
proclaim the name Yahweh is the Old Testament equivalent of
confessing saving faith in the Lord Jesus Christ in our own day.

To such persons comes the promise of God that there will
be salvation to the survivors of the greatly terrible Day of
Yahweh. That salvation will center in Mount Zion, Jerusalem.
For it is there that the center of the new kingdom will be
established. Moreover, there is a nice *inclusio* on the word "to
call" in this verse. Joel 2:32 opens with the words, "everyone
who calls on the name Yahweh," and then ends, "whom Yahweh
calls." That is, there is an interrelationship of the call of man to
God and the call of man by God. From one whom God calls,
there will be the responsive call to God. Here is a delicate
blending of the biblical teaching on the effective call of God and
the response of faith demanded by the one to whom God's call
comes. This issue of the call *of* God and one's call *to* God is
complex, one of the most debated issues in theology. But Joel
presents the two notions in juxtaposition. One thing is certain:
in the mind of our great God there is no confusion on the issues
of divine election and human responsibility.

This Is What

When Peter spoke to his deeply curious hearers that
Pentecost Sunday morning, he quoted the words of the prophet
Joel. He said that the wonders they were observing among the
people of Jesus were the very wonders this Old Testament text
prophesied: "This is what was spoken by the prophet Joel"
(Acts 2:16).

The question that faces all interpreters of Joel 2 and of Acts 2 concerns how much of "this" is "what." That is, in what way may we say the prophecy of Joel was fulfilled in the experience of those early believers during the Pentecost experience.

We may list some particulars:

- Certainly the principal issue in both texts is the outpouring of the Holy Spirit upon the people of God. We may assume with confidence that the outpouring of the Holy Spirit to the small band of believers in Jesus came without reference to sex, age, or class. That is, women spoke along with men; younger people, along with older; servile, with free.

- Second, the outpouring of the Spirit in both Joel 2 and Acts 2 is associated with spiritual gifts of unusual forms of speech. The prophecies, dreams, and visions of Joel 2 became the speaking in other languages in Acts 2; there is a close tie in the fact that both texts deal with speaking gifts.

- Third, the outpouring of the Holy Spirit on Pentecost was associated with some heavenly phenomena and with certain paraphysical signs. We think again of the mysterious windlike sounds and the marvelous firelike tongues of Acts 2:2–3).

- Fourth, the outpouring of the Holy Spirit on the day of Pentecost was a time of tremendous evangelism. Acts 2:41 says that about three thousand were added to the small number of disciples and believers in Jesus on that one day. This is a stunning harvest of the Spirit, a mark of the reality of his power among these people.

- Fifth, there is a proper geographical center from both texts; they both center in the city of Jerusalem. The Holy City of Jerusalem was the scene of the death and resurrection of the Savior Jesus. It is appropriate that it is also the place of the pouring out of the Spirit of God on the people of God. Jerusalem will also be the center of the coming kingdom of God.

This last phrasing helps us to think of things that are

dissimilar between the oracle of Joel and the fulfillment in the experience of the apostles.

- The special wonders and omens in the heavens and on the earth that Joel prophesied (2:30–31) were not realized except minimally. Either Joel's language is bombastic for rhetorical effect, or there is more to come from the prophecy at another time. There is a sense in which the observer of Acts 2 might have asked about the rest of the signs and omens.
- The notable egalitarianism of Joel 2 is only partially realized in Acts 2 and following. While we certainly may assume that younger and older, male and female, servile and free persons were active participants in the events of that grand day, this sense of a profound change in role restrictions is not commented on in Acts 2. Nor is it a realization in the years that followed in the early history and teaching of the church. Only occasionally do we read texts, such as Galatians 3:28 and Colossians 3:11, that seem to relate more to the equality of the standing of all persons before Christ, rather than to the equality of opportunity for spiritual ministries of the spoken word. As is well known, some New Testament texts seem to put severe limitations on women in vocal, teaching ministries in the local church (see 1 Tim. 2:11–15). A continuing controversy is provoked by comparing these several texts. But in these controversies, it would seem appropriate that Joel 2:28–29 must be considered.
- Third, the major difference between the expectation we have in Joel 2 and the realization we find in Acts 2 concerns the concept of the time of the end and the association of the prophecy with the coming of the Day of Yahweh. There is a sense in which we may say that the Lord Jesus Christ initiated the time of the end in his ministry. He came preaching the kingdom of God, the kingdom of heaven on earth. But the full realization of the coming of Christ's kingdom on this earth is still future. The Day of Yahweh is still future. We still await that day.

Fulfillment

These areas of congruity and discongruity between the prophecies of Joel 2 and the fulfillment of Acts 2 lead us to the discovery that there is a complexity in the ways in which such a biblical prophecy may be fulfilled.

We hear the words of Peter in Acts that the prophecy of Joel was being fulfilled before the eyes and ears of all the people of Jerusalem. We believe Peter, and we give assent that Joel 2 was fulfilled on the day of Pentecost—for it was fulfilled.

Nonetheless, not all of the details of the prophecy were fulfilled that day. There were not the wonders in the heavens, not the coming of the Day of Yahweh, not the establishment of the kingdom, not the drastic and final changes in society we might have hoped. But these days are coming. These fulfillments are ahead. One day the prophecy will be filled to the full.

Biblical prophecy may be pictured as having a conical shape extending from the Old Testament occasion on the left, to the fully-opened bell with the kingdom of Jesus Christ on earth on the right. All along the way there may be fulfillment. It is all a part of the same prophecy.

In the case of the prophecy of Joel 2:28–32, we may see one of the great fulfillments of this text on Pentecost with the outpouring of the Spirit on the saints in Jerusalem. But there were other outpourings of the Spirit in the Book of Acts. These, too, were fulfillments of Joel 2. There have been grand occasions of the work of the Spirit of God in the extending of the community of faith. These are also fulfillments of Joel 2:32, which speaks of the prominence of the salvation work of God in association with the coming of the Spirit.

And in a still future day of God's great grace, there will be the ultimate fulfillment of all that Joel saw so long ago. This will be in the final battle, the coming of the King, the establishment of the kingdom of the Savior, and the incomparable blessings of the people who will come to salvation all along the prophetic line.

Surely, we who live between these great fulfillments of Joel

2, from Pentecost until the coming of Christ's kingdom, should live in expectancy.

We should also live with eyes open and ears ready. The King is coming and so is the age of righteousness and the fullness of the Spirit. One might not have thought that a small, "minor" prophet such as Joel would have had so much to say on such grand themes.

For Further Study

1. Compare the phenomena of nature accompanying God's revelation of himself during the formation of his people Israel at Mt. Sinai (Exodus 19-20) with the phenomena associated with the formation of his people—the Church—in Jerusalem (Acts 2).

2. Compare and contrast the exact wording of Joel 2:28-32 with Peter's quotation in Acts 2:17-21 in your Bible. How similar or dissimilar are they?

3. What are other great *Old Testament* texts that speak of the reality, work, and Person of the Spirit of God? Use a Bible concordance and look under the word "Spirit."

4. How may the inclusion of *women* in the Spirit's gifting of Joel 2 relate to the issues of male/female roles in the church today? Or is there a relationship? Can you defend your answer? Does your answer include the data of Joel 2?

5. Can you point to other Old Testament prophetic texts in which fulfillment shows similar congruity and lack of congruity as the relationship of Joel 2 and Acts 2 presents?

Chapter 9

War in the Valley of Decision
(Joel 3:1–16)

Final Battle

It is not unusual for those with a casual knowledge of the biblical concept of the final battle to think that this great conflict will be a world war between the superpowers. What most people think of when they hear the word "Armageddon" is an all-out nuclear conflict between the United States and the Soviet Union.

When we come to the biblical descriptions of the final battle, however, we may find ourselves somewhat surprised to learn that the final battle is not the conflict between the great superpowers of the world. The biblical prophets do not speak of a time when warheads from Kansas silos will be unleashed against the cities of Russia, or the warheads of Soviet subs against the heartlands of America.

Final battle concerns the armies of God against the armies of man. Final battle, Armageddon, is the battle of Yahweh, not the battle of men. It is the battle of Yahweh against the nations assembled together against Jerusalem and Israel to destroy God's people and to thwart the reign of God's Son, Y'shua, on the throne of David. Numerous prophetic texts in Scripture describe this final battle. Psalms 2 and 110 present these issues in poetry. Revelation 19 does so in apocalyptic prose. Joel 3:1–16 is just one of the great texts from the Hebrew prophets on this terrible subject.

97

Time Setting

Joel 3:1, (4:1 Hebrew, see preceding chapter) begins with a time reference that helps us to understand something of the historical setting for the outworking of this prophecy.

"In those days and at that time,
    when I restore the fortunes of Judah and Jerusalem."

Here are words of God's future work on behalf of the people who were presently under distress. These words drive us back to the preceding text, to the time period of Joel 2:28–32 (3:1–5, Hebrew). As we have seen, Joel 2:28–32 is set in the time of the end, for it in turn is dependent upon the far future placement of the events of Joel 2:18–27. All of the second half of the Book of Joel (from 2:18 through 3:21) is in the future tense from Joel's perspective, and most of the contents of this text remains in the future tense from our own as well.

Restore the Fortunes

Joel 3:1 ends in the telltale phrasing, " 'When I restore the fortunes of Judah and Jerusalem,' " an indicator of the time sphere of the activities of this section. This phrase may also be translated, "when I bring back the captives," as in the NKJV. Scholars continue to debate the primary meaning of the words of this phrasing, but the intent is clear. When Yahweh restores the people of Judah and Jerusalem to their land, in fulfillment of his ancient promise, then he will have restored the fortunes of his people.

This promise of future regathering was first given by Moses when he told the second generation to leave Egypt just as they were about to enter the land of promise for the first time as a national entity. Moses told them of the sin and rebellion that would mark the lives of their descendants and the resultant wrath of Yahweh that would drive them from their land (Deut. 29:25–28). Then he speaks of the eventual return of the people of Israel to the land of their fathers, at at time when they return to Yahweh with full integrity and under his renewed compassion (Deut. 30:1–10). The phrase that we find in Joel 3:1 occurs in Deuteronomy 30:3, "then Yahweh your God will restore your fortunes," or, "then Yahweh your God will return your captives" (see marginal note, NIV, and text of NKJV).

This is the prophetic climax, yet it was part of the original promise. Yahweh's plan for Israel was clearly delineated by Yahweh through Moses from the very beginning. There remain secret things to God, but there are innumerable things that God has revealed to us and belong to us and to our children forever (Deut. 29:29). The prophecy of the final restoration of the Lord's people Israel to his land and to this blessing is among the revealed things.

It is also a favorite topic of the prophets. Zephaniah 3:20 is an especially lovely text that uses the same phrasing as Joel 3:1 and Deuteronomy 30:3. Jeremiah in particular is most expressive concerning the resolute plan of Yahweh to restore his people Israel to their place and his pride, a special development of chapters 30–33 of his book. Further, it is possible that Joel was contemporary with Jeremiah and Zephaniah, as we have noted in the introduction. Those prophets who ministered near the very end of Judah's existence had a strengthened hope for the work of Yahweh to continue in this beyond exile to restoration.

It is especially important to see Jeremiah and Zephaniah using this phrasing, for these prophets whose prophetic ministry began in the same year 627 B.C. lived during the final stages of Judah's apostasy. Joel's dating is still in dispute, but the dating of these prophets is certain. If Yahweh were to change his mind concerning his beloved people when they had presented such egregious sins, certainly he would change his mind through the prophets Jeremiah and Zephaniah.

Not so, however. Jeremiah 30 is one of the most impassioned prophecies of the future regathering of Israel from among the nations. The thesis is stated in verse 3, with the phrasing we have seen in Joel 3:1. The elaboration is exquisitely moving, culminating in the words of the great bonding of God and man, " 'So you will be my people, / and I will be your God' " (Jer. 30:22). Chapter 31 of Jeremiah adds more luster to the promise of final deliverance, leading to the promise of a new covenant that Yahweh will establish with his renewed people (v. 31). Truly, only if the decrees by which Yahweh governs the universe were to disappear in an instant, only then would the descendants of Israel ever possibly cease to be his people (vv. 35–37; see also Jer. 32:44; 33:6–9; 33:11, 26, and wider contexts).

Is it any wonder that the apostle Paul writes as he does in Romans 9–11? The reason there is a coming time when the people of Israel will finally be saved (Rom. 11:26) is found in the revealed things of God that go all the way back to the Book of Deuteronomy. Here is basic biblical doctrine, but so little known or appreciated in our day.

 Joel 3:1 presents the time of the prophecy of this chapter in the context of the time of Yahweh's final regathering of his people in the land of his promise. Joel 3:1 is not a specific date, such as a circled number on a calendar, but its general sense in the time sphere of the prophetic hope is well recognized in Scripture.

Into the Valley

The prophet Joel now recounts the words of Yahweh to bring all nations into the Valley of Jehoshaphat to face final judgment (Joel 3:2). The word "Jehoshaphat" means "Yahweh judges." This name of one of the kings of Judah is used here to describe what type of encounter Yahweh is about to bring upon the nations. He brings them before him as guilty ones for judgment; he brings them to "Judgment Valley."

Elsewhere, we read that the Lord will bring about the final conflict in the Valley of Armageddon (Rev. 16:16), also known as the Valley of Jezreel. The term "Armageddon" is derived from Hebrew *har megiddo*, Mount Megiddo, that magnificent promontory that guards the major north-south highway on the west side of the great Valley of Jezreel.

Many have written about the suitability for a battle field that Armageddon, or the Valley of Jezreel, affords. Some writers, for example, like to quote Napoleon who is said to have remarked on the admirable use this location would provide for a major battle.

And what battles there have been here! Innumerable battles have been fought on this plain, and some may be fought there again.

It is not necessary, however, to localize specifically the final battle into the confines of this magnificent, but still limited, valley in the north of Israel. The prophets speak of final battles in terms of the wars they knew. While they wrote of the future, they had to write in such a way so their first audience would know what they were describing. Wars in the times of the prophets were fought by armies facing each other on local, limited battle plains in hand-to-hand combat, with horses and chariots, with swords and spears.

Were the final battle to be fought in our own day, we presume it would be with modern weapons and with sophisticated, up-to-date technology. We also presume that though there might be a primary battle area, this war would be global in nature. "Armageddon" speaks more of a kind of battle than a place for the war.

There is no place on a map that we may identify as the "Valley of Jehoshaphat." We may understand that the prophet had in mind somewhere near the city of Jerusalem, but there really is no clearly identified site with this name. The two deep valleys we see at Jerusalem today, the Valley of Hinnom to the southwest and the Valley of the Kidron to the southeast, could hardly fit the battle scene. Moreover, in verse 14 the prophet calls the location of the battle "The Valley of Decision." Clearly, Joel is focusing on the etymological meaning of these words rather than directing us to a location on a map. This is a common way of the prophets, to see in words the special meaning from the root or associated ideas to form a spiritual double-entendre, a significant play on words.

"The Valley of Jehoshaphat" is the Valley where Yahweh judges; it is "Judgment Valley." "The Valley of Decision" is the Valley where Yahweh pronounces his sharp decision, "Decision Gulch." Final battle is the issue.

These several words—Armageddon, Jezreel, Jehoshaphat, and Decision—all refer to the same sort of thing: There will be a locus for the final battle which will be under the control of God. It will be he who will bring all his foes to a central location and will there bring about their ruin. That locus will be the place where Yahweh will judge (Jehoshaphat Valley), the place where he will bring his decision (Decision Gulch), the place where God will plant (Valley of Jezreel; see Hos. 1:4, 11; 2:22).

To the Bar

The call of God is for the nations to come before him for judgment. The scene in Joel 3 is a familiar one in the prophets. Scholars call this the *rîb*motif, based upon a Hebrew word for the judicial imagery, sometimes translated "a charge" (see Hos. 4:1 and Mic. 6:2.) The particular term *rîb*is not used here in Joel 3, but the notion is certainly present in the Hebrew verb "to judge" found both in the symbolic name, "Valley of Jehoshaphat," and the words, " 'I will enter into judgment' " (Joel 3:2). The specific charge of Yahweh against the nations in this text is their abuse and mistreatment of his people Israel and of the land that was his heritage for them. God will repay the nations for their repeated and incessant ill-treatment of his own.

The imagery used by the Lord in verse 3 is truly shocking. Imagine the callous disregard for life, for personhood and dignity as to trade away a boy for a few tawdry moments with a prostitute, to bargain away a girl for a drink of wine. This drastic use of language is an assault to our senses, but not to ours alone. This language presents the abuse of his people as an assault to the senses of God.

I Call Philistia

Joel 3:4–8 presents a particular instance of the abuse of the people of God by their enemies Phoenicia and Philistia. It is not just that this case is exceptional; it is also a sample of the way the nations had regularly abused the Hebrew people. On all such acts of abuse comes the expected judgment of God.

These concepts go all the way back to the beginning, to Yahweh's covenant with Abram. The words of Genesis 12:3, " 'and whoever curses you I will curse,' " are dramatic and incisive. This poetic colon might be paraphrased and expanded somewhat, "and any individual [the Hebrew is singular here] who regards you as insignificant or who treats you in a demeaning or trifling manner [the Hebrew verb means, "to treat lightly, to make light of"], such a one I shall bring under my strongest curse [the Hebrew verb is different than in the first part of the colon; it is a much stronger word].

The Lord's words to Phoenicia and Philistia are words of retaliation that are particularly suited for their crimes against humanity. These peoples treated with contempt the children of Israel, so shall their children be severely treated. There is a poetic justice to the retribution of God upon these ancient enemy nations of Israel. The punishment is in kind. The nations are representative of the nations as a whole. In the time of final judgment it will be all the nations against the bar of Yahweh.

We are not certain of the time period and nature of the abusive actions of Phoenicia and Philistia against the temple and the people of Jerusalem that Joel has in mind, beginning in verse 4. It seems likely that these actions were in conjunction with the destruction of the city of Jerusalem by the Babylonians for other defeated or allied peoples took part in the Babylonian ruin of the holy city.

The participation of other nations surrounding Judah in the fall and destruction of Jerusalem is a particular concern of the prophets. Obadiah, for example, wrote his bitter prophetic word against Edom for her dreadful participation in the rape of Jerusalem. Phoenicia and Philistia may have been co-conspirators in the Babylonian attack on the holy city, the despoiling of holy things, and the ruination of the children. Joel could have written these words in anticipation of their actions, by the prophetic stance of the work of the Spirit. He might also have written these words shortly after the fall of the city, as an eyewitness of the events along with Jeremiah.

In any event, the message is clear: God is about to bring calamity on their own heads; he is also about to bring his people home. These two contrasting items are the principal issues: the enemy will be judged, and God's people will come home.

The Trumpet Call for War

Joel next portrays the sounding of the battle cry for the nations (3:9–13): "Prepare for war!" There appears to be something of a sarcastic irony in these verses. Joel reports God's call for soldiers to be awakened, for implements of agriculture to be made into weapons of war, for weaklings to boast of their strength, and for all this motley crew to assemble together at his command.

This section may be a prophetic and poetic development of the scornful derision of Yahweh at the petty state of his puny foes in Psalm 2:4. These nations are inspired by Satan, emboldened by the Beast and empowered by the false prophet, as the Book of Revelation presents. Nonetheless, it is a preposterous idea that all the nations of earth with all the power of modern weaponry would have a chance at dethroning the Creator of the universe, or of forestalling his King, the Lord Y'shua!

And so God laughs, and his attendants avert their glances.

The words of Joel 3:10 seem to be a deliberate inversion of Isaiah 2:4 and Micah 4:3. In those two texts, which are anticipative of the blessings of the millennial kingdom, there will no longer be the necessity for nations to stockpile massive arms against future wars, for war will be a thing of the past. The implements of warfare may be transformed into implements of agriculture. Here are great passages for peace!

But in Joel 3 it is not a time for peace; the battle is still ahead. The prophet spurs on the opposition. But he also calls for Yahweh and his armies to join the battle (v. 11, last colon). And so we notice again that the final battle is between Yahweh and the nations. Any other warring between and among the nations, terrible as they are, are minor skirmishes compared to the nations coming to Judgment Valley. Here all generals come to their Waterloo; all commanders meet their Nemesis; each warrior, his better. The enemy is Yahweh, an enemy they have made by persecution of his people.

Harvest Time

The Book of Joel repeatedly uses agricultural imagery, and not surprisingly, the locust invasion in the time of the prophet was a devastation that animates the book as a whole. In Joel 2:24, we have read of the abundant agricultural increase that Yahweh will bring to his people in a coming day of plenty. There the threshing of grain and the flowing of grape juice are the most pleasant of themes. These words speak of tranquility, peace, and prosperity.

What a contrast we find in Joel 3:13! Now the imagery of

harvesting has been transposed to the judgment of God upon the nations. Now whitened fields of wheat call for the judgmental sickle, and the abusive actions at the threshing floor. Now freshly picked clumps of grapes invite the crushing, stomping, grinding feet that will smash away until nothing is left but the dried out pulp.

The call for the harvesters of grain and for the stompers of grapes is not pleasant at all in this text, and this presents a significant switch from what we usually think. We are long accustomed to speak of the fields that are white unto harvest for the gospel mission, as the Lord Jesus described in Matthew 9:37–38. He spoke with urgency concerning a harvest of life, a lifting for redemption.

But the harvest of Joel 3:13 is of another sort: here is a harvest for destruction. The sickles are in hand, the sandals are removed from many feet, the end is near for the enemies of God.

We are not surprised to find John building on similar themes as he describes the final battle in Revelation 19:11–21. There John speaks of the trampling out the vintage of his terrible swift wrath (v. 15).

The stomping of grapes in a vat, a rock trough, is an image then that may present two very different pictures in our minds. One is the joy that the harvesters feel as they have the harvest in and are now breaking the grapes, releasing the juice, and anticipating the filling of their vats with the wine, which is so often a symbol of the joy of living. Another picture we get is quite opposite: this is the image of the spattering of juice, the discoloring of garments—it is as though the stompers of grapes have been at war. Joel uses both images, joy (2:24) and war (3:13).

One terrible day there will come the commands of God, "Swing the sickle! Stomp the grapes! Now's the time. My day is now present!"

Battle and Deliverance

Joel 3:14–16 describes the climax of the battle Yahweh wages with the enemies of his people, and the deliverance he offers for his own.

The numbers involved may be the saddest aspect to all of

this. Joel 3:14 envisions a great number of people who have been called to Decision Gulch. "Multitudes, multitudes"—the words suggest innumerable people. That so many would share the fate of God's wrath is especially troubling to us, or ought to be. For surely it is grievous to God to think of the numbers of wicked persons involved in resisting his will, in mistreating his people, and in rejecting his grace.

It may sound old-fashioned and unfavorable in our day of possibility thinking, but the fear of God's judgment on wicked persons ought to stir the righteous not only to guard their own walk, but especially to be involved in the rescue operation of delivering fools from their folly. There is little room for possibility thinking when one is an enemy of Yahweh.

Again in Joel 3:14 we read the words, "the Day of Yahweh." The Day of Yahweh has come near in Decision Valley; it is here realized. The Hebrew word translated "decision" comes from a word meaning "to cut, to sharpen, to decide." This word progresses in meaning and in use from that which indicates the use of a cutting instrument, to the making of a sharp, incisive decision. Here Yahweh will make his sharp decision of judgment. The Valley of Decision is another term for the Valley of Jehoshaphat (3:2, 12). Both of these words refer to the actions of God in the judgment of the nations.

In Joel 2:10 we read of the trembling of the sky, the darkening of the sun and moon, and the withholding of light by the stars. This was in the setting of the advancing armies who were coming against Jerusalem like locusts had invaded the land. Again in Joel 2:31 we read of omens in the heavens associated with the coming Day of Yahweh. Joel 3:15 presents the same imagery. Heaven itself is convulsed at the judgment activities of Yahweh. This is why Joel speaks of the darkness of the day (2:2). The natural lights of God's heavens become unnaturally dark; over the earth comes a ghastly pale.

And then there is the sound, the sound of his roar! (v. 16). As a lion, Yahweh gives forth his voice; the sound of his voice is as thunder from Jerusalem (see 2:11). And all heaven seems to shrink back in fear. The pictorial language of these verses is designed to cause the reader to wince, to feel the sensation, to hear the voice, to image the event. Poetry is the language of experience. Joel the prophet uses his poetic gifts to bring his readers to hear the day, to smell the acrid odor of the judgment of God.

At the same time, as is so common with the prophets, in the midst of the most excruciating of judgments, Joel brings in again a picture of the mercy of Yahweh to his own people, of the grace of God to those who are faithful to him in the crisis.

> But Yahweh will be a refuge for his people,
> a stronghold for the people of Israel
> (3:16, last couplet).

Here is the language of pure grace, an experience of his love, a sense of his deliverance. With this part of the verse a believer's thoughts may rush to the opening verses of Psalm 91, which speak so eloquently of the hiding place in God, of dwelling in the shelter of Shaddai. The prophets share this image. Zephaniah 2:3 also presents the picture of the protection of God's people in the midst of his overwhelming judgment.

With these words, we are now prepared for the final section of the book, Joel 3:17–21.

For Further Study

1. Read Deuteronomy 29-30 and trace the history of Israel up to Moses' day, following the prophetic outworking of Israel's future destiny. Note how many prophetic themes we discover in Joel that first are seen in this text from the Torah.

2. Now read Jeremiah 30 and see how it ties to both Deuteronomy 29-30 and to Joel 3.

3. Use a good Bible atlas to locate and identify Megiddo, the Valley of Jezreel, Philistia (with its five principal cities), and Phoenicia (with its two principal cities).

4. The Hebrew word *rîb*, (*charge* or *legal suit*) sounds like *reeve*. This word is characteristic of prophetic speech in announcing the judgment of God. Read Hosea 4 for an example.

5. Review the changes in Joel to agriculture resulting from natural calamity, divine judgment, and then divine restoration.

Chapter 10

When Yahweh Dwells in Zion
(Joel 3:17–21)

Prophetic Burnout

We need to face the fact that we live in a period of prophetic burnout. There was so much interest in biblical prophecy of end-time events a few years ago that some people really are not interested much any longer. They feel that things got out of proportion. There are some people who become more concerned with identifying the foes of the beast than knowing or practicing the fruit of the Spirit. Too many preachers titled their sermons like the headlines of a supermarket tabloid rather than with a regard to the biblical godliness of themselves or their people.

Some in the prophetic minicraze of the seventies not only lost a sense of proportion, they even became disobedient to the very prophecies they were proclaiming. The Savior Jesus himself insisted that of the specific time of the end, of his return and the establishment of his kingdom, no one knows, not the angels, nor even the Son of Man in his humanity, only the Father (Matt. 24:36). Yet book after book in our own day pretentiously and rebelliously pretends to know the things Jesus forbade them to presume.

The result has been something of a turning away from prophetic themes on the part of many people.

Some have wondered whether it would have been a relevant thing to the people who first read these words to have extended sections of biblical prophecy cast into the far and dim future. "What does an extended discussion of the acts of God in the far future have to do with the lives of people living in ancient times?" modern scholars sometimes ask. Further, these people often say that the prophets are "forthtellers" more than they are "foretellers." They are far more concerned with the sins of the people of their own day than they have an interest in the affairs of people in a distant day.

We may observe that there is some justification to these criticisms. In the prophecy craze among evangelical Christians in the 1970s, there was a disproportionate attention given to the future predictive prophecies of the Old Testament prophets. There was also a benign neglect of the principal messages of these prophets for repentance and righteousness addressed to the people of Israel and Judah, and by extension, to believers who would hear these words of the Lord in our day.

At the same time, the prophets do set their own agendas, under the hand of God. It is not uncharacteristic at all for the prophets to move from their own present to a far and distant day. Sometimes they do this only at the end of their books and much more briefly than in the message concerning their own generation. Amos, for example, comes to a prophecy of the end times only in the very conclusion of his book (Amos 9:11-15). The rest of that book was addressed to the people in the times in which they lived. The proportion of end-times prophecy in Amos is very slight; unfortunately, this has led to a neglect of the study of Amos among those students of biblical prophecy who were only concerned with end time texts.

We may observe a contrary experience. Those who feel the prophets speak only to their own times are prone to dismiss the last part of Amos as nonauthentic. What we need, of course, is a sense of balance.

Joel gives us his message as he received it from God. He does begin in his own present, as we repeatedly noticed in our reading of his description of the locust invasion. But he soon thrusts his own message into the time of the end, for the present experience of his people was seen by the prophet as a splendid teaching device for end-time understanding.

As to the question of relevance of a knowledge of end-time events for a people who had to live their own lives a long time ago, we may simply observe that there is always an issue of the relevance of such prophecies throughout the history of Israel and the church. That is, why should anyone care about end-time texts?

Why should we care?

The End of the Story

On reflection, we may answer. We care, as did people in ancient times, because we desire to know the outcome of injustice and evil and the prospects for righteousness and hope for peace. It makes a difference in our own lives, and in the lives of believers who lived in the days of the prophets, to know that one day, at last, there will be a divine judgment of evil, there will be a redressing of wrong, there will be a flourishing of right. As there was a beginning and a middle to the story of evil, so will there be an end. The Bible does not present its story with no ending as is done in some modern nihilistic novels. There will be an end, and that end gives the whole story its meaning.

In fact, it is only with a divinely given hope for the final victory of right over wrong that we, and those who have lived before us in the continuity of the faithful community, may relieve our sense of frustration at the ambiguity, uncertainty and enigma of our own existence. Unexpected, unexplained evils that come into our own lives, be they locusts or disease, war or disaster, are placed in a divine perspective when we have some knowledge of God's future dealings with evil itself. Further, the demands of righteousness in the lives of believers are magnified with a proper sense of final judgment.

Finally, we may simply observe that predictive prophecy is a grand part of the teaching of Scripture. Prophecy exists not so much to answer speculative questions as to suggest there are answers that will be forthcoming. Prophecy exists not so much to tell us "when," as to tell us "that." Time lines that are too specific may undermine the basic intention of predictive prophecy in the Bible. Our focus is not to be so much on the exact determination of when such and such should occur, so much as on the nature of the occurrence, the righteousness of God, and the eventual coming of his kingdom.

His Dwelling

We turn now to the last section of the Book of Joel, verses 17–21, where we find this prophet's magnificent description of the end hope of biblical prophecy. The ultimate hope of the prophets, as God spoke through them, was not something esoteric or fantastic, not something eerie or speculative. The prophets reach out for a day when God dwells with man and man with God in the joy of his presence.

Here is significance for any age. People who first heard these words, we who read them now, and all believers who have stretched from then to now—we need to know that right will out, that God will reign, that peace will come.

We are to be deeply impressed with the words of verse 17 as the direction toward which the book has resolutely been moving.

> "Then you will know that I, Yahweh your God,
>   dwell in Zion, my holy hill.
> Jerusalem will be holy;
>   never again will foreigners invade her."

To know God rightly is a major teaching of the Scripture. Indeed, it was in large part to present a more intimate knowledge of God that the Savior became man (see John 1:18). He who had dwelt in the utmost intimacy with the Father through all eternity became man so that as man he might more fully explain what it means to know the Father.

And in becoming man, the Savior Jesus "dwelt among us" (John 1:14, NIV). The Greek word in the Gospel of John translated "lived for awhile" is akin to the Hebrew word we find in our Book of Joel, "dwell." Both words speak of God making his residence among mankind. The Hebrew verb is *shākan*, "to settle down, to abide, to dwell." It occurs twice in the last section of Joel, in verse 17 and at the end of verse 21. This double use is an *inclusio* as we have seen earlier in our study, a device that serves to frame these verses into a unit. Both times the specific form of the word is *shōkēn*, the present participle form, meaning that Yahweh "is dwelling" in Zion. In this case, it is not just living for a while; Joel speaks of an ongoing dwelling of God with man (see also v. 20).

Joel shares a common vision with his possible contemporary, the Hebrew prophet Zephaniah. One of the loveliest verses in all Hebrew Scripture is Zephaniah 3:17. I particularly love the expression of the intent of this verse in the NKJV:

> Yahweh your God in your midst,
> The Mighty One, will save;
> He will rejoice over you with gladness,
> He will quiet you with His love,
> He will rejoice over you with singing.

There it is! Yahweh in the midst of his people, the One who has come to save them is now co-resident with them. And his presence is in great joy, a calming presence, even a singing presence! So speaks the prophet Zephaniah. And so speaks Joel of Jerusalem in 3:17 of his prophecy.

In these words Joel stretches beyond the first coming of the Savior Jesus Christ, his passion, resurrection, and ascension. He grips in his vision the central message of the second coming of Jesus. Indeed, Joel of Jerusalem stretches all the way to the vision of John in the Revelation of the coming of the new heavens and the new earth. Joel sees the presence of God with man, he hears much the same words as John the disciple heard from an heavenly presence saying,

" 'Now the dwelling of God is with men, and he will live with them. They will be his people, and God himself will be with them and be their God' " (Rev. 21:3).

Not only does Joel see the dwelling of God with man, he sees as well the coming of the holy city of Jerusalem. As with the prophet Zechariah, Joel knows that Yahweh will one day again choose the city of Jerusalem for his dwelling place and for the locus of the outpouring of his blessing (Zech. 1:17). Joel says, " 'Zion, my holy hill,' " and " 'Jerusalem will be holy' " (3:17). As we have observed on 2:1, the term Zion may be used as a synonym for the city of Jerusalem. In Joel 2:1 Zion was the place for the sounding of the trumpet of alarm. In 3:17 Zion is the holy hill, the temple mount, the very dwelling place of God with man.

Joel also adds that there will never again be strangers who

will traverse the land. The land will be home to those who know the Lord. Those who are strangers, foreigners, or invaders will not come here again. The land is now holy to Yahweh, set aside to his holy purpose and to his holy presence. The city is distinct. It is holy.

John sees much the same thing. John describes his vision of that city this way, "I saw the Holy City, the new Jerusalem, coming down out of heaven from God, prepared as a bride beautifully dressed for her husband" (Rev. 21:2). The words of John accord with the words of Joel.

The vision of Joel is wonderful on its own merit. That it reaches to the end of the New Testament revelation is stunning.

His Name

Joel's words also focus upon the name of God in this grand verse of his coming to dwell with his people: " 'Yahweh your God.' " There is something quite satisfying to the reader to see this emphasis on the name of God at the climax of Joel's book. For, as we noted in the introductory sections, the name "Joel" means "Yahweh is God." How truly lovely to find the message of the book and the meaning of the name of the prophet coming together in this way.

The name of the prophet was given to him by his parents, or perhaps by the midwives attending his birth. That name then was an attestation of the faith of those who chose that name for him. But the one who matured bearing the name "Joel / Yahweh is God" learned to live it out as the genuine expression of his own character and his personal faith in God. Not all beautiful names are borne by beautiful people. But here are a name and a man matched for each other, and providentially designed for the one who would write this little book.

His Land

A second feature that Joel wishes to impress on his readers is not only that the end time will be characterized by the personal presence of God with his people in the holy city of Jerusalem; also, there will be a dramatic change in productivity of the land in the time of his presence (see also, Ps. 65).

How interesting that a book beginning with an account of an

insurmountable agricultural disaster, ends with a descriptive passage predicting an overwhelming agricultural renewal. This section is the fulfillment of God's original intent to bring great blessing to his people through the land of Canaan. But it is more than fulfillment; it is promise itself. One day the land will be Eden redivivus, paradise regained. One day the land will be all that God intended for his land before ever a rebellious man and woman dared to challenge him on his own ground.

One day (some readers may need to take a breath here) there will be an abundance of new wine. Joel writes in verse 18, "'the mountains will *drip* new wine.'" The Hebrew word is *nāṭap,* a word used in just the same way in the vision of Amos (see Amos 9:13). The balancing words of verse 18 present an abundance of milk and water, "'and the hills will flow with milk; all the ravines of Judah will run with water.'" These are pictures of plenty, portraits of joy. The active, expressive verbs add vitality to the picture. Wine presents the establishment of the vineyards once more. Milk presumes the goats and cattle needed for production. And water gives meaning to the whole, particularly in the arid land, which is so very dependent upon the rainfall and the waterbrooks.

What a reversal this picture in 3:18 is from the desperate plight of the citizens of Jerusalem in Joel's day, when he was seeking out even the drunks to awaken and weep because there would be no more wine for them in coming days (see Joel 1:5). The priests were to join the drunks in lamentation, since they would also suffer terrible lack of the elements of their worship (1:9). Drunks and priests were to be joined in mourning by farmers and vine growers (1:11); joy was stripped from the land as a blanket is seized from a bed. Indeed, joy and gladness had withered away with the last green leaf of the locust invasion.

But a new day is coming. A day is coming when the mountains will be alive with the sounds of vineyard workers, the hills abundant with the lushest of grapes, and new wine luxuriating down the mountain slopes, as honey dripping from a spoon. The association of wine with milk and water in a context of blessing demands a positive posture on Joel's part for using these words this way. These words give us an exquisite expression of the wonder of the nearness of God. Wine is often used this way in the Bible as a symbol of joy, and the lack of wine as a symbol of the loss of joy; there is no greater joy than to be in the presence of God.

The River of Life

The new day also has a new watercourse:

> "A fountain will flow out of Yahweh's house
> and will water the valley of acacias"
> (3:18, last couplet).

These words drive us ahead again to the Revelation of John. For he also speaks of a new watercourse that emanates from the very throne of God in the midst of his new city (Rev. 22:1, 2). John terms this stream "the river of the water of life," describes it as crystal clear, and speaks of it as coursing down the very middle of the great street of the city, and watering numerous trees. Joel speaks of this same river; he even mentions the trees!

The Fate of the Enemies

Joel 3:19 speaks of the terrible ending of the nations who repulse Israel, who violated her dignity, and who killed innocent people of Judah. All such enemies, be they Egypt or Edom, will end up desolate, as desert wastes. This is a part of the divine retribution we never should forget in these texts. God will bring on the heads of the enemies the very sort of thing they attempt to bring on the head of his people. Egypt and Edom are singled out here as representative nations. Egypt is to the south and Edom to the southeast of Israel. And these nations, like Phoenicia and Philistia (3:4), were constant in their attack on the people of Israel and their land. One day they will suffer the worst of evils, their very lands will become as a desert, whereas the land of Israel will be a place for blossoms to grow.

And the End?

To know the end is to know how to walk today. It makes all the difference in the world to deal with a problem knowing that there is a solution, rather than to deal with the problem and not know at all that there even is an end. It makes all the difference in the world to know that there is a story going on in God's world, and that this story has a true beginning, a genuine central section, and a finely honed ending; against supposing that perhaps all of life is transitory and all meaning is relative.

To know the end is in some way to know God.

Jerusalem Forever

Joel 3:20 explains that the new Jerusalem is not a passing thing. It abides forever, joyfully inhabited by the people of God, and wondrously indwelt by the person of God.

The sins of the people of God will finally be pardoned (3:21); their bloodguilt will not last forever. In fact, we know that the final solution for the problem of sin was made by the atoning death of the Lord Jesus Christ (Rom. 4:25). It was that death of the Savior that satisfied fully the demands of God in view of the enormity of sin. No longer is God angry, Joel says. Now he pardons.

The Book of Joel ends with the words of his heart,

Yahweh dwells in Zion!

Those who read these words are drawn as well to the words of the prophet John one more time as we remember how he responds to the similar prophetic vision. His familiar words from Revelation 22:20 end his message, and our book:

Amen. Come, Lord Jesus.

For Further Study

1. Reflect on the proportion given in the Book of Joel to end-time events as against contemporary events. Then read quickly through the book of Amos and observe the proportion of those events there.

2. Read John 1:1-18 and compare the "dwelling" of Jesus in his first advent with the dwelling of God that is still future from Joel 3:17-18.

3. Note that even at the end of the book, themes of judgment and mercy interplay. Compare Revelation 22.

Resources for Further Study

There are numerous commentaries available on the minor prophets in general and on the book of Joel in particular. Doubtless your church librarian or your local Christian bookstore will be able to point you to some that will help. In evaluating a commentary for your use, read a sample section to estimate the level of complexity of discussion. Some commentaries are designed for specialists; others are written more for the general reader. Also, you will want to get some sense of the perspective of the writer, especially in terms of his or her commitment to the integrity of the word of God.

More important than commentaries, however, for your own study are books that will enable you to do your own research. These books include a thorough Bible concordance. This should agree with the Bible translation you are using. There are fine new concordances for the New International Version as well as older concordances for other translations.

You should also have access to a thorough, reliable Bible dictionary. Some are one-volume editions, and others come in multi-volume sets. Look for recent publication dates, signs of reverent scholarship, and accessible information. You may also wish to use a resource for understanding Hebrew words. Here I suggest the *Theological Wordbook of the Old Testament* by Harris, Archer, and Waltke (Moody Press). You may access this dictionary by the Strong Concordance numbers, a set of numbers published with an increasing number of Bible study tools.

Finally, you will wish to have access to a good Bible atlas

that has numerous perspectives of events and topography. The land of Palestine (modern Israel) could be the most carefully studied parcel of land on earth. It ought to be studied well by you, also.